MW01616544

Many of us have com ... *ways in this country* ... *new churches. Few peop...* ~~have carried the respect in church planting~~ *as Tony Merida. This book will enable those planting churches, or wondering if they should, to benefit from the wisdom and experience of one who of the key leaders of the church planting movement today. If you care about church planting, you will come away from this book with a kind of coaching and mentorship that can only come from one with this sort of earned credibility and authority and fidelity.*

Russell Moore, Public Theologian, Christianity Today

The Faithful Church Planter *by my friend Tony Merida sees through the "cool" church planter image that has let us down. Tony guides us back to what we really believe. This book will help raise up a new generation of faithful and fruitful church planters who deserve to be celebrated and supported.*

Ray Ortlund, Renewal Ministries, Nashville

As I read through the eleven church planter competencies outlined in this book, I found myself wishing it had been written thirty years ago so that I, a "somewhat healthy" church planter, could have been healthier in my own church planting efforts. So often church planters get distracted from the things that are primary (godly character and the fruit of the Spirit) by things that are secondary (growing an organization and having impact). To borrow a word play from C.S. Lewis, "Aim at character and you'll get impact thrown in; aim at impact and you'll get neither." I can't recommend this book highly enough not only for church planters, but also for every pastor and ministry leader. It's essential reading.

Scott Sauls, Senior Pastor of Christ Presbyterian Church; author of *Jesus Outside the Lines* and *A Gentle Answer*.

The Faithful Church Planter *is a must-read for anyone whose heart beats for the Great Commission work of church planting. If you want to plant healthy churches that make and multiply disciples, a healthy church planter is critical. Tony Merida provides an invaluable framework for how to assess church planters that is biblically sound, both concretely practical and heart-stirringly inspirational, all-the-while remaining accessible to both the pulpit and the pews. This resource needs to be in every pastor, planter, and aspiring planter's hands as they follow God in this holy calling.*

Dr. Doug Logan, Jr. President of Grimké Seminary and Dean of Grimké Urban; Associate Director of the Acts 29 Network; author of *On the Block: Developing a Biblical Picture for Missional Engagement*

There are a lot of books that have been written on church planting. However, too often they simply focus on nuts and bolts at the expense of the character and calling of the planter. I am pleased to commend to you The Faithful Church Planter *by Tony Merida which contains gems to be found for those who are prayerfully considering the work of church planting.*

Dr. Winfield Bevins, Director of Church Planting, Asbury Seminary; author of *Marks of a Movement*

A healthy church multiples – it plants new churches. This book by Tony Merida would be an excellent one for a pastor to walk through with a growing leader who aspires to help lead one of those new plants. Because being able to plant takes more than just a desire to do so, but the grace-given competencies to do so well to the glory of God.

Scott Zeller, Executive Pastor of Redeemer Church of Dubai; Network Director, Acts 29 Emerging Regions

The title of this book says it all. Acts 29 exists so that healthy churches are planted by faithful church-planters. The 11 competencies in this

book are a solid foundation, and Tony Merdia does an excellent job of showing the biblical roots and the practical fruit of these qualities. This book is challenging and encouraging, practical and principled, timely and timeless.

Philip Moore, Associate Director, Acts 29 Global; Network Director, Acts 29 Europe

As I read this book I found my affections for the church, church planting, the lost and Jesus stirred anew.

Tony has done a great job in giving clear biblical foundation and direction for thinking through these essential competencies for church planting and church leadership. A work I'm sure will be revisited time and time again as we train and send people for the glory of Jesus. I can't wait to take all our planters and leaders through it.

Steve Robinson, Senior Pastor, Cornerstone Church, Liverpool; Director, Cornerstone Collective

We've likely heard the statistics on church planting and pastoral longevity; few would disagree that ministry in the twenty-first century is becoming increasingly complicated. More than ever we need a Spirit-powered faithfulness to Jesus, his Word, his Church, and his mission. That's why I'm so glad Tony has written this book. Tony writes as a seasoned pastor, exploring what we should look for in a potential church planter and their team, so that may run well and run long in the race that God has set before us. Here you will find a biblically-faithful, gospel-soaked, treasure chest of practical wisdom. I want to put this book in the hands of every aspiring church planter exploring their calling, as well as every church leadership team who desire to send out healthy, multiplying churches. Highly recommend!

Adam Ramsey, Lead Pastor at Liberti Church, Gold Coast, Australia; Network Director for Acts 29 Australia, New Zealand & Japan; author, *Truth on Fire: Gazing at God until Your Heart Sings*

Here is sound, biblically-grounded, and very practical instruction. The Faithful Church Planter is chock-full of both keen insight and necessary reminder. If you are anticipating church planting, either as a planter or as a sending church, this book will point you clearly in the right direction.

Mike Bullmore, Senior Pastor, CrossWay Community Church, Bristol, Wisconsin

Church planting is a scary leap of faith. Church planters, their families, and their teams wonder if they're doing it right, if they're rightly honoring the Lord, if they're going to make it to the other side. Written, not as a how-to manual, but as a helpful guide for the journey, Tony Merida offers us wisdom, clarity, and true encouragement. By combining his own experience with that of countless other church planters who he's helped along the way, Merida removes some of the mystery and mystique from the call to church planting. While it is Jesus alone who builds his church, this book will be a tremendous service to planters as they evaluate their own context, gifts, skills, and calling to the local church.

Jen Oshman, Jen Oshman, author of *Enough About Me*; church planter's wife, Redemption Parker; podcaster; women's ministry leader

With his many years of pastoral and church planting experience, Tony Merida provides a treasure-trove of balanced wisdom in this manual for church planters. He insightfully recognizes that those called to this challenging work not only need specific ministry competencies but must also have godly character. This is why any church leader serving Christ's church will benefit from reading this book. So, if you've been gripped by the amazing grace of God, and want to see it transform the lives of those around you, listen and learn.

Julius J. Kim, PhD, President of The Gospel Coalition.

If you want to plant a church, start with this book. Tony Merida is a master synthesizer and expositor. He can take a complex, massive topic like church planting and provide a succinct, biblical guide. I wish I could put this book in the hands of every aspiring church planter.

Adam Muhtaseb, Pastor for Preaching and Vision,
Redemption City Church

The Faithful Church Planter

The Faithful Church Planter

Eleven Essential Competencies for the Work

Tony Merida

Unless otherwise stated, Scripture quotations are from The Holy Bible, English
Standard Version ESV®. Text Edition: 2016. Copyright © 2001 by Crossway Bibles,
a publishing ministry of Good News Publishers.

Copyright © 2021 by Tony Merida

First published in Great Britain in 2021

British Library Cataloguing in Publication Data
A record for this book is available from the British Library

ISBN: 978-1-783973-25-5

Designed and typeset by Pete Barnsley (CreativeHoot.com)

Evangelical Press (EP Books), an imprint of 10Publishing
Unit C, Tomlinson Road, Leyland, PR25 2DY, England

www.epbooks.org
epbooks@10ofthose.com

1 3 5 7 10 8 6 4 2

Contents

Foreword

If it had been left to me (and thank goodness it was not) to choose a single word to capture the essence, the mindset even of the pastor who authored this book and the church planting network he serves, I would make the case for *fruitful.* Yes, fruitful would have been my word choice. And perhaps the choice of others as well. After all, Tony Merida and the Acts 29 Network he helps bolster are equally known for producing overflowing baskets of gospel fruit. Fruitfulness in the form of healthy churches planted and newly born Christians established. Even now, more than 700 churches around the globe are developing as well-connected gospel vines from the fertile soil of this affiliation. The abundance of this spiritual fruit is the remarkable work of God. It is eminently worthy of our celebration, as well as our ongoing intercession.

I could imagine a phrase like *the fruitful planter*, on first glance anyway, serving well to convey my initial perception. But here, in the pages you are about to read, a stronger descriptor of both the man and the movement is put forward, one more perfect in substance – I am referring to *faithful.* Stated more expansively, *The Faithful Church Planter*. Tony Merida opts for this better choice.

For *faithful* more fully embodies what those of us who have planted churches must ultimately be after. Don't get me wrong, we all desire fruit. But we must yearn for fruit that emerges from being faithful.

Without this overt concern for fidelity to the gospel stated upfront – *faithfulness* as that which governs the mindset of every would-be church planter – many ministers and ministries have suffered in our time. In fact, it is precisely because Pastor Merida chose to write to us about faithfulness, not mere fruitfulness, that your mindset and mine have a fighting chance to be nurtured in better soil. Tuck this truth away. For Merida's insight instructs even before you get out there to go grow something good for God. To put my opening commendation for this volume plainly, I am excited for you to read this book because it will instill foremost in the mind of the church planter the mindset of Christ. I long for emerging pastors to better know what they are setting out to become while planting a church. *The Faithful Church Planter* will help.

Between the front and back covers of this volume you will find Merida explicating eleven competencies. Think of them as part skills, part aptitudes, but when taken together these eleven comprise what Acts 29 is looking for in a church planter. By way of method then, each competency gets its own chapter. And so, you hold in your hands a guide to acquiring pastoral proficiencies.

The most important thing I can say about the book's methodology goes beyond asking you to work hard at storing all eleven elements in your long-term memory, as though the intent of Merida's method was for you to be able to call them to mind in some future ministerial moment of need (an impossible feat anyway). No, the better point to take on Merida's methodology is the manner in which he accomplishes his ends. Each chapter adopts a style that comes close to sermonic form. To put it bluntly, in each chapter Merida takes a text of Scripture (usually from the letters of Paul, but on occasion from one of Peter's epistles, and at least once from the very words of Jesus) and from them he simply expounds.

The advantage of this method is striking for any church planter. You will be more firmly convinced in the power of the Word preached. And believe me, the methodology of the book relies simply on a straight-forward handling of God's Word. Oh, that more church planters would adopt this same method in establishing their congregation. Far too often men head into ministry doing something other than exposition. Yet here, you will be challenged and strengthened by the Word itself, wonderfully executed through Merida's pastoral voice. I remain incredibly grateful for the chance this book gave me to sit under the preaching of its author. And my hope is that you will take hold of this same method to establish your ministry.

Having put down some thoughts on Merida's mindset and methodology, it remains only for me to say what came to mean the most to me. The book put forward really good pastoral models. I was struck while reading *The Faithful Church Planter* with just how often it was the

Apostle Paul himself, not merely the things he wrote, that became the measuring rod for my own progress. The force of Paul in these pages is aimed at *imitatio*. In fact, Paul is so pervasively employed in the text that you will see him in every chapter (even on the one on marriage!).

With these models then, the book moves from principles you are to fix in your mind to persons you can see, observe, and learn to follow. And isn't this exactly what someone who desires to plant a church needs? We need examples to follow, not only outlooks to absorb. And Merida gave us, in Paul, the greatest church planting pastor, the one to emulate. But in these pages Paul does not stand alone. In two chapters at least, another worthy model is espoused. The author's employment of Peter is also meant to stir you toward greater faithfulness. And Jesus stands out in this work supporting them both. Remember, none of us who have planted churches do so on our own. Merida doesn't. And neither do the pastors in the network he serves. Thank God for models.

Enough from me. Let me turn you over to Tony. For the mindset he espouses is spot on. The method he champions is right. And the models he provides are worthy. This is a book to read and come back to. And it is one that I pray will be used by God to keep you faithful to the end.

David R. Helm
Senior Pastor, Christ Church Chicago
Chairman, Charles Simeon Trust

Introduction

One of the joys of my ministry career has been training aspiring church planters around the world. For instance, in Kiev, Ukraine, I had the privilege of teaching a group of church planters at Kiev Theological Seminary each year for about fifteen years. The church-planting program was started by my friend Joel (now retired and living in Indiana), who had a vision for seeing churches planted across the former Soviet Union. One of my favorite memories was when we were doing student introductions and testimonies. A brother named Emmanuel, a massive man from Lithuania who had spent time in prison, shared about his rough, former life. He said that the only time he opened a Bible in those days was to use its pages to smoke various substances, but now he's opening the Bible to preach it! How do you go from smoking the Bible to preaching the Bible?

It's because Jesus Christ saves sinners (1 Tim. 1:15). Due to Christ's work in his heart, Emmanuel became a humble and gentle leader.

God can change the most hard-edged sinners, the vilest men and women, and turn them into ambassadors for Christ (2 Cor. 5:20). He took Paul from being a terrorist to being a pioneer evangelist and church planter (Gal. 1:11–23). And God is still doing this transforming work today. Sure, one may not have a history in prison, or a story exactly like Paul's. Still, everyone's story is powerful because God has taken those who were spiritually dead and made us alive together with Christ (Eph. 2:1–9).

When I'm talking to strangers, this question often comes up: "So what do you do?" I love to have them guess; they almost never guess "pastor." I then like to tell them, "I'm more surprised than you are!" The grace of God truly is stunning.

The fact is that you never know from where the next great ministry leader may come. He may be a rebellious church kid right now, or a freshman at your local college, or the little hipster at the coffee shop, or the high-school kid who is sneaking off campus to smoke e-cigs. Jesus Christ can take a mess of a person and turn them into a messenger of life. That's because the gospel still works. It still is the power of God unto salvation (Rom. 1:16). As church planters and ministry leaders, we must have an unshakable confidence in the gospel.

What makes a church planter?

In addition to being a converted person, a church planter needs to have some other essential qualities. While many of the traits of a church planter are similar to the qualifications for pastoral ministry in general, there are some distinct gifts, skills, and experiences found in church planters. The eleven competencies identified here are the current competencies that we use at Acts 29 for assessing church planters. This list contains a good bit of overlap, but I believe it's valuable to address each one respectively. Others have identified more than eleven traits of a church planter, but we have found these particular competencies to serve church plants and church-planting teams well.[1] This concise book is intended to give an introduction to each one.

The primary audience for this book is church planters, but much will apply to those on church-planting or church-ministry teams. I have tried to flatten my application in various places where the principles apply to a broader audience. Pastors of established churches may also benefit from this book, as we consider the work of pastoral ministry throughout. Finally, faithful church members are encouraged to read along as well, since many have never read or studied about church planting in detail. A book like this will bring clarity to the church's mission, will show how everyone can in some way engage in church planting, and may even ignite a passion for being part of a new work.

Faithful leaders planting healthy, multiplying communities

The aim of this book is not merely to provide another collection on a bookshelf or to transfer some information. It is to inspire and instruct in such a way that more healthy leaders are able to plant more healthy churches. We need millions of equipped church planters and church-planting teams to be deployed across the globe, scattering gospel communities everywhere.

By planting churches, we have the privilege of being in on God's sovereign work in the world. God's redemptive plan has always involved having a people for himself (Tit. 2:14; 1 Pet. 2:9–10). When you start a church, you're doing more than starting an event at a storefront, a school, under a tree, in a house, or at some other location. You're actually participating in this grand narrative of God having a people for himself (Acts 18:10), a story that culminates in John's glorious vision in Revelation where a people from every tribe and language and people and nation are giving praise to the Lamb (Rev. 5:1–14). This vision compels us to be faithful in our present generation until the mission is finished.

We get to carry on the Great Commission that Jesus gave us—a task that itself points to church planting. As we go about making disciples among the nations, we are told to do this by *baptizing* and *teaching*, which we see happening in the context of the church (Acts 2:41–47). New believers need to be discipled by faithful pastors and leaders, who will also train and send out more healthy leaders to plant multiplying churches.

Church planting is the air you breathe when you open the New Testament, as the New Testament is largely written to a collection of church plants. In the book of Acts, we read of the origin of several of them. We get to carry on this vision, as Acts 29 people. What a privilege to be part of this work. What responsibility we have for seeing to it that we are planting and leading healthy, multiplying churches. We have been given a great stewardship.

Our sufficiency is from God

Finally, let me give a word of encouragement. A competency list like the one found in this book can seem overwhelming. You may be led to ask yourself, "Who is sufficient for these things?" (2 Cor. 2:16).[2] The apostle Paul not only raised that question but answered it: "Not that we are sufficient in ourselves to claim anything as coming from us, but our sufficiency is from God, who made us sufficient to be ministers of a new covenant" (2 Cor. 3:5–6a). Paul recognized his sufficiency (or "competency," CSB) came from God. We are not sufficient, but our God is. Left to our own resources, we fall short. But our confidence is in the fact that God's grace and power are enough. Ultimately, it is God who makes us competent. He makes a church planter. So we say with Paul: "Now to him who is able to do above and beyond all that we ask or think according to the power that works in us—to him be glory in the church and in Christ Jesus to all generations, forever and ever. Amen" (Eph. 3:20–21, CSB).

1

Spiritual Vitality

Spiritual vitality is the result of the gracious work of God in raising men and women from death to life, giving them a living, vibrant faith. As those who have been raised with Christ by the Spirit, we have the privilege of walking by the Spirit in this world, displaying the fruit of the Spirit in our character, and fruitfulness in our ministry.

There are many elements of spiritual vitality that one could discuss, including (but not limited to):

- The new birth and its effects (John 3:3; 1 Pet. 1:3–2:3)

- Union with Christ (Rom. 6:1–11)

- Being transformed by the Spirit (2 Cor. 3:18)

- Confessing sin regularly (Jam. 5:16)

- Rejoicing with grateful worship (Phil. 4:4)

- Being in meaningful community with other believers (Acts 2:42–47)

- Being committed to the authority of Scripture in life and ministry, and the regular meditation

on Scripture for growing in sanctification
(2 Tim. 3:16–17; Col. 3:16)

- Having a vibrant prayer life (Rom. 12:12)
- Walking by the Spirit and displaying the fruit of
the Spirit (Gal. 5:16–26)
- Resisting the temptations of the evil one (Jam. 4:7)

Like "vital signs" show how well one's physical body is
functioning, these kinds of experiences show how healthy
one's spiritual life is.

For the purpose of this chapter, I would like simply
to apply Paul's words in Ephesians 6 about spiritual
warfare, as many of the above items are touched on in
this important text, and I think it's especially relevant for
church planters and pastors.[3]

Church planters are desperate for God's power

When pastor Tim Keller decided to leave a respected
seminary to go plant a church in New York City, he
described the experience this way:

*[I] felt totally inadequate for the job [planting Redeemer
Presbyterian Church]. I know that everyone feels
inadequate for any ministry, but this was different. I
knew that I was as humanly well-equipped as anyone to
try this ministry, but I also knew this was well beyond the
human abilities of anyone at all. That meant only one*

thing for me: it would not be my talent, <u>but my love for,</u>
<u>and dependence on, God that would be the critical factor</u>
<u>in the project.</u> I felt that my spirituality would be laid bare
for all (worst of all, for me) to see … I prayed and was
reading Gurnall's A Christian in Complete Armour
one day and came upon a passage: "It requires more
prowess and greatness of spirit <u>to obey God faithfully</u>
than to command an army of men; more greatness to be
a Christian than a captain." I realized that it was an
illusion to imagine that I would have to start being brave
if I took this job [planting Redeemer]; I should have been
living bravely all along. Even if I turned the NYC church
down, I could not go back to being a coward. So I might
as well go to New York! On July 1, I gave Westminster
Seminary a year's notice. Immediately, my prayer life
broke open like never before *(my emphasis).*[4]

Church planting should cause your prayer life to break open
if you consider how hard it is, and what kind of warfare is
involved. We go with faith in and reliance on God.

I'm not suggesting that you can't be a prayer warrior
if you aren't a church planter (that would exclude many
Christians!). I simply mean it will challenge you in ways
that bring you to your knees with longer times in prayer,
it will take you on longer prayer walks as you pour out
your heart to God, and it will bring you together with
others for prayer more than normal. Every church planter
and church-planting team member that is assessing things
properly should be able to resonate with Jehoshaphat's

prayer: "For we are powerless against this great horde that is coming against us. We do not know what to do, but our eyes are on you" (2 Chr. 20:12).

We are powerless, but we can stand in the Lord's mighty power. If we don't, we won't withstand the attacks of the evil one. Our strength is not in our giftedness, in our age, in our biblical knowledge, or in our ministry experience. Our strength, this very moment, comes from our union with Christ and is supercharged by our communion with Christ (cf. 2 Tim. 2:1). We live out of our weakness and into the Lord's strength (cf. Heb. 11:32–34).

The war we face

Even though it's not popular to talk about "warfare" in various parts of the world today, one cannot miss the emphasis in Scripture on this theme, from Genesis 3 onward. This passage in Ephesians 6 is rooted in the Old Testament. While Paul is certainly aware of Roman soldiers, and maybe even looking at them at the time of writing, his language is more influenced by the majestic warfare imagery of the Old Testament, especially from Isaiah.

The Old Testament often refers to God (and his Messiah) as a warrior and his people as "troops" who are in need of God's strength (cf. Ex. 15:3; Ps. 18:39; 35:1–3; Isa. 42:13; 52:7). Further, God and his Messiah also wear these items mentioned in Ephesians 6 (Isa. 11:5; 49:2). These echoes and allusions point us to the very nature of our Messiah and his power. The armor given to us is his own armor. To put on the armor of God is to put on the Messiah himself. It means to be identified with him, and to fight with his strength, displaying his character.

Christ has already triumphed over the powers of darkness, but we have not yet experienced the fullness of Christ's victory. The battle still rages for Satan knows his days are short (Rev. 12:12).

This connection of Ephesians 6:10–20 to the rest of the letter is important because it shows us various ways in which this warfare is waged. In the immediate context of 4:1–6:9, Paul spoke about ethical and relational challenges, but in Ephesians 6, he points us to the cosmic and spiritual battle that exists. Our relational challenges in the church, our challenges in the home, or our public witness in society are complex, and one of the reasons for them is the reality of spiritual warfare.

As servants in Christ's church, we shouldn't be surprised by warfare in every arena of life. As one writer puts it, "It is Satan's desire to divide and destroy the Christian church, the family of God, and the family unit of human beings. He would love to sidetrack, discourage, or effectively negate all Christian ministry. ... Satan can successfully steal our encouragement, our confidence, and our joy. His tools include doubt, injury, unforgiveness, and disappointment."[5] Indeed, the devil has many "schemes" (Eph. 6:11), and many "designs." So let us live in light of this reality, and let us rely on God's power to persevere in faithfulness.

THE FAITHFUL CHURCH PLANTER

Paul also points out that the evil one *wrestles* (6:12). The battle is up close and intense. The devil is not firing laser-guided missiles from a distance; he is upon us. Jesus told Peter, "Satan demanded to have you, that he might sift you like wheat, but I have prayed for you that your faith may not fail (Luke 22:31–32). Even though conflict includes physical people and physical dangers, there is an unseen battle that we face. We wrestle against "rulers, against the authorities, against the cosmic powers over this present darkness, against the spiritual forces of evil in the heavenly places" (Eph. 6:12b). This speaks to the dark powers that work with the evil one.

Paul is writing to Christians in general, but it's imperative for planters and pastors to remember they're Christians before they're ministry people. This means that we too must always beware of "the evil day" (6:13). I take this evil day to refer to the present evil age we are in (5:16) and of *particularly tempting occasions*. Consider Matthew 4:11 and the phrase "then the devil left him." The devil on this particular occasion came with great force to destroy Jesus. He will come in particularly strong ways on particular occasions to tempt us, as well. Therefore, we must stand strong by God's power.

Put on the full armor of God

The three imperatives in Ephesians 6:10–11 are "be strong in the Lord," "put on the whole armor of God," and "stand." Notice also the repetition that follows: "stand"

(6:11), "withstand" (6:13), "stand firm" (6:13), and "stand, therefore" (6:14).

So there is a *defensive* element in spiritual warfare: stand, holding your ground. Don't yield to Satan's temptations and don't listen to his lies. Resist him by God's power. And James adds, "He will flee from you" (Jam. 4:7b). We also have an *offensive* responsibility: to take up "the sword of the Spirit" (Eph. 6:17). Just as we would not dream of going into battle without a weapon, we should never envision engaging in mission without being strapped with the Word of God.

Fortunately, we don't fight this battle alone. Along with our fellow believers, we're to be "striving side by side for the faith of the gospel" (Phil. 1:27). We support, pray, and build up our fellow soldiers.

After telling us to put on the armor, Paul now describes it. We don't wear sweatpants or holiday clothes; we wear battle gear.

Belt of truth (6:14a)

The devil loves to tempt planters and ministry leaders to lie, cheat, and manipulate people. Resist this temptation, remaining a person of truth. Live and minister with "simplicity and godly sincerity" (2 Cor. 1:12). By God's grace, resolve to lead with the absence of duplicity or deviousness. Live above reproach by being a minister who speaks the truth of the gospel, and one whose "yes" is "yes" and whose "no" is "no" (Matt. 5:37).

Breastplate of righteousness (6:14b)

Once again, we are to put on the virtues of our Messiah (cf. Isa. 59:17). This refers not to imputed righteousness (our right standing before God) but to practical righteousness. By the power of the Spirit, we are to live in a way that accords with the new identity we have in Christ. Don't give an inch to Satan in the areas of lust, greed, or impurity (cf. Eph. 5:3). Many pastors will be tempted in these areas.

Gospel shoes (6:15)

Paul says, "As shoes for your feet, having put on the readiness given by the gospel of peace" (Eph. 6:15). Today, one can find shoes for almost any kind of activity. Historians tell us that the Romans were issued superior footwear than their enemies. With their studded half-boots, they marched great distances in all kinds of terrain. Like these soldiers, church planters go into hard places, ready to share the gospel with everyone at all times (cf. Isa. 52:7).

Shield of faith (6:16)

The word Paul uses for "shield" is a big shield that covered the whole body. In Scripture, God is referred to as our shield (Ps. 18:30; 28:7; Prov. 30:5). Praise God that we have a shield to protect us from the enemy's arrows! Let us pray for one another that we would look to God to be our refuge, and not to a counterfeit refuge. He alone is our shield.

Helmet of salvation (6:17a)

The idea here is that we regularly put on the hope we have in the gospel, being assured of our salvation (cf. Isa. 59:17; 1 Thes. 5:8). Don't let the enemy get in your head, but instead rehearse the gospel daily through Scripture reading, prayer, and song; taste the goodness of the gospel in the Lord's Supper; remember your baptism when others are baptized.

Sword of the Spirit (6:17a)

This term refers to a short sword or dagger, used in up-close combat. Paul normally uses *logos* for "word," but here he uses *rhema*, which usually refers to the spoken word. If that is the case, then he is referring to speaking the word in a particular moment. Again, one hears echoes from Isaiah here about the Messiah (Isa. 11:4; 49:2; cf. Rev. 19:15). We are given access to the weaponry of the Messiah for battle when we are united with him. Don't look at the Bible as an ancient sword in a museum—as useless for modern battle. See it as absolutely necessary for engaging in the battle. Read it. Meditate on it. Sing it. Pray it. Proclaim it.

Be devoted to prayer

Paul does not begin a new sentence in Ephesians 6:18, but rather continues his exposition of this spiritual warfare. He adds to his teaching that we stand firm against the enemy's schemes through *prayer*.

Unlike the other items previously mentioned, prayer is not associated with a piece of armor or equipment.

However, one may think of it as a soldier's line of communication with headquarters. John Piper has referred to prayer as a "wartime walkie-talkie." That's not the only way to envision prayer, but it works when thinking about spiritual warfare. It is such a gift to be able to call up and say, "Help!"

When Paul says, "praying at all times in the Spirit," he means all true prayer is by the Spirit. And because of the gift of the Spirit, the Christian warrior has constant access to God in the midst of the war (2:18; cf. 3:16; Jude 20; Rom. 8:26).

Notice also the four universals to express the comprehensiveness of prayer (Eph. 6:18). We pray "at *all* times"—when we rise, when we work, when we play, when we eat, when we hang out together, and when we lie down. We pray "with *all* prayer and supplication." That is, we are devoted to prayer for ourselves, for others, for our church, for the advance of the gospel, for the welfare of the city. We do this by staying "alert with *all* perseverance." Recall how Jesus urged the disciples to "watch and pray" in light of temptation (Mark 14:38). We read about persistence and perseverance in prayer elsewhere in the New Testament (Acts 2:42; 4:23–31; 6:4; 12:5; Rom. 12:12; Col. 4:2). As church planters and ministry leaders, we have to keep prayer as a priority in the life of our church, as we make supplication "for *all* the saints."

We should never feel embarrassed to ask for prayer. Instead, remember that even the mighty apostle Paul requested prayer in order that he may boldly and effectively communicate the gospel (Eph. 6:19–20). All of our evangelistic efforts, as "ambassadors for Christ," are to be done prayerfully. Evangelism is spiritual warfare, and we need God's Spirit to be faithful witnesses in this dark world.

Conclusion

Spiritual vitality refers to our spiritual life as Christians. Our new life in the Spirit is a gift granted to us by God, as people who have experienced the new birth. While we cannot lose this life, that doesn't mean there's no battle. On the contrary, life and ministry are envisioned in Ephesians 6 as spiritual warfare. Church planters and ministry leaders must be aware of this battle, rely on the Lord's strength, walk in God's armor, and look to God in prayer, in order to be faithful ambassadors for Christ.

Reflection questions

1. What spiritual "vital signs" could you point to that would demonstrate your communion with Christ?

   In reading over the list on pgs. 11–12 I believe all of them are present and I'm growing in them. I need to grow in my disciplined consistency, however.

2. How are you seeing God answer your prayers?

   Providing strength to my spirit, in the midst of so much darkness

3. How are you experiencing the power of Christ in your life and ministry?

   His strength, because I would keel over and die trying to do what I do if He didn't help me.

4. Consider your own wartime stance (Eph. 6:10–20)—how are you being strengthened by God

(6:10), putting on the whole armor of God (6:11, 13), holding your ground against the enemy's schemes (6:11, 13, 16), and prayerfully engaging in evangelistic mission (6:17–20)?

I'm teaching through John, need to be more constant in prayer + Word. I'm not going into sm. Spreading gospel at work and on trip to people of El Salvador.

2

Theological Clarity

Faithful church planters and pastors desire to saturate the nations with sound doctrine. Therefore, having theological clarity in one's teaching and leadership is essential. There are many doctrinal points we could underscore for doing this, but I want to reflect on the need for being committed to *gospel centrality* in life and ministry.

In parts of the world, particularly in the West, we are trying to reach atheists and agnostics who are quite secular in their thinking and apathetic when it comes to religion. There are many happy pagans we're trying to reach. However, in other parts of the world, the problem is not trying to get irreligious people interested in divine things, but rather providing theological clarity for already religious people. I have seen all sorts of religious practices around the world today, but sadly, many of them are Christ-less practices.

Being gospel-centered

I recall being in Kenya and chatting with my friend Femi Osunnuyi, a fellow Acts 29 pastor in Lagos, Nigeria. We were talking about the need for doctrinal precision and gospel centrality in his context. At an Acts 29 event, pastor Femi gave a very helpful grid for understanding gospel centrality, differentiating it with other alternatives.

Gospel-denying churches

Various cults and extreme brands of liberalism would fit this category. They deny the essential truths of the gospel, and therefore shouldn't be called a church.

Gospel-redefining churches

These churches add to or subtract from the gospel. Examples include the prosperity gospel and the social gospel, or Jesus + religions.

Gospel-assuming churches

These churches believe the gospel, but they rarely preach it plainly and deeply. They may not deny substitutionary atonement on a doctrinal statement, but it's not communicated explicitly and regularly in preaching and discipleship. They're kind of *Christianity lite*. Sermons are filled with self-help ideas, ways to be better parents, how to manage finances, and so on, making them hard to distinguish from the wisdom of the age.

Gospel-affirming churches

Like the previous group, these churches may actually adhere to the gospel on paper, but the gospel is seen as being only for evangelism. As such, it's also not communicated directly in gatherings, but is reserved for outreach ministries.

Gospel-proclaiming churches

These churches are a great improvement. They are known for preaching the gospel every week in gatherings, but the gospel is still primarily viewed as that which is simply evangelistic. While the gospel is viewed as the reason for worship, and so their songs are often very rich in gospel doctrine, many in these churches still see the gospel mainly as that which gets one to heaven. That leaves the question of *what happens after a person is converted?* The critique of this kind of church is that the gospel is often neglected in ongoing discipleship. Instead, what is often emphasized is some kind of moralistic behavior (devoid of grace) and a particular way of thinking about culture, which includes (but isn't limited to) a particular political and social ideology.

Gospel-centered churches

These churches preach the gospel explicitly every week, but *not just for the unbeliever.* The gospel is viewed as that which brings the dead to life, and that which then shapes and empowers Christian ethics and the life of the Christian community. When ethics are taken up, the gospel is applied. Marriage is taught by looking at Christ's love for the church (Eph. 5:25ff.); generosity is viewed through the lens of Christ's generosity (2 Cor. 8:9); the call to forgive is rooted in Christ's forgiveness for us (Col.

3:13); hospitality reflects the welcome of Christ (Rom. 15:7). Social ministries like orphan care, widow care, refugee care, and care for the poor are motived by the grace and mercy we have received from God.

First Corinthians is another great book to consider gospel-centered leadership. At the beginning, Paul says he knows nothing but Christ crucified (1 Cor. 1–2). Then in chapter 15, Paul glories in the resurrection. In between chapters 1 and 15, Paul talks about many subjects (lawsuits, church discipline, sexual ethics, and more). But every topic is to be viewed through the lens of the good news of what the crucified and risen Christ has done for us, and all that our Christ has for us.

Further, gospel-centered churches place a value on the grand drama of Scripture. The Scriptures are like a treasure map that leads to Jesus, the promised Messiah. And finding gold leads to joy! The categories and themes like prophet, priest, king, mediator, temple, sacrifice, the second Adam, the promise to Abraham, the Son of David, the Son of Man, the Son of God, the Servant of the Lord, the Messiah, the King, the Redeemer, the Savior—all of these and more—are fulfilled in Jesus (cf. John 5:39, 46; Luke 4:20–21; 24:27, 44). All the promises of God find their "yes" in Christ (2 Cor. 1:20). Seeing Christ in all the Scriptures is vital for our evangelism, but also for our discipling Christians. As Christians behold our Savior, they experience glorious transformation (cf. 2 Cor. 3:18).

The wonder of the biblical narrative

At the center of the story are the events of Easter. D. A. Carson says, "The whole Bible pivots on one weekend outside of Jerusalem."[6] The message of Easter is the best news in the world! The centrality of this weekend is illustrated by how much focus the gospel writers put on the week of Jesus' Passion. It's also illustrated by how the Apostle's Creed jumps from Jesus' birth to his suffering, crucifixion, and resurrection, with nothing said about his life. There's a reason we make a big deal about Easter: if these things didn't happen, we should call the whole thing off (1 Cor. 15:12–20). Christ has died, he has risen, and he will come again. A healthy church never loses the wonder of the good news.

While recognizing the beautiful diversity of Scripture, and the diamond-like quality of the gospel, Tim Keller contends, "At the heart of all of the biblical writers' theology is *redemption through substitution*" (my emphasis).[7] The story of the Lamb inspires awe and praise. Sam Allberry summarized some of the story like this:

- Genesis 22: a lamb for one man

- Exodus 12: a lamb for a family

- Leviticus 16: a lamb for the nation

- John 1: a lamb for the whole world[8]

When John called Jesus this Lamb of God (John 1:29), he had the Old Testament hopes in view. And how does this theme appear later in Revelation? With redeemed sinners from around the globe singing, "Worthy is the Lamb who was slain, to receive power and wealth and wisdom and might and honor and glory and blessing!" (Rev. 5:12).

This redemptive work of Christ is the fountainhead for every spiritual blessing we have as Christians. It's why we need the Bible. There is a sense in which one can understand that there's a Creator apart from Scripture. Passages like Romans 1:18–25 speak of this *general revelation*. But you can't get from a pine cone to propitiation (creation to the atonement) without *specific revelation (Scripture)*![9] It's this good news that transforms sinners and makes us people of hope and joy.

A church member once approached her pastor and said that she couldn't quite understand how the Bible was a unified story. The wise pastor grabbed an envelope and sketched the storyline of Scripture in the following six symbols.[10]

The Story of Scripture

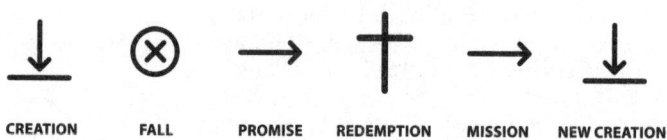

| CREATION | FALL | PROMISE | REDEMPTION | MISSION | NEW CREATION |

One could easily draw this overview on a napkin or teach it to children.

The arrow coming down in *creation* refers to the first two chapters of the Bible, as we read of God creating the world. God also created the whole space-time universe, but the emphasis in Genesis is how God created the world in which we live.[11] The X symbol refers to Genesis 3 and is meant to symbolize *the fall*. The effects of sin entering the world are seen immediately in Genesis 4–11. The arrow pointing to the right symbolizing *promise* primarily represents God's promise to Abraham. God promised to bless the world through Abraham's family—which happened in Jesus the Messiah. However, we should remember that the promise is as old as Genesis 3:15, where redemption is promised immediately after the fall. There, God promises to send one (through the woman's offspring) to crush the head of the serpent— which happened through Jesus the Messiah. The cross symbol is meant to represent all that we find in the gospel narratives, with the life, ministry, death, resurrection, and ascension of Jesus. It represents *the good news* of great joy: the good news of what God has done for sinners through Christ. The next arrow pointing to the right includes *the mission* of the church, which begins in the book of Acts and continues through us today. The final downward arrow represents *Christ's return and the new creation* (cf. Rev. 21–22). We read of no more sin, death, sorrow, tears, or fears, but of God dwelling with his people forever.[12]

Some simplify the storyline of Scripture to four stages (*creation, fall, redemption,* and *new creation*). Others like to show the link between the *covenants*, referring to the grand promises God made in the Bible. We read of his covenant with *Noah,* and then with *Abraham.* We also read of the covenant at *Sinai,* and then his covenant with *David.* Finally, we arrive at the *new covenant*, foretold by the prophets and inaugurated by Jesus. Covenants are wonderful ways of showing people that God keeps his promises!

We need some kind of outline in our minds to tell the gospel story to people. I also love for people to read the story of Stephen (Acts 7:1–53) and Paul's sermon at Antioch in Pisidia (Acts 13:16–41) to show biblical examples of the narration of Scripture. (Keep in mind, though, that these are speaking to a Jewish audience. Consequently, they do not argue the early part of the story, namely creation and fall, but rather begin with Abraham and Israel.)

We should remember the value of being able to retell the story of Scripture for both evangelistic and discipleship purposes. Concerning *evangelism,* the unity of the Bible helps unbelievers understand the whole context of Christianity, rather than just the little controversial bits that many of them know. My wife, Kimberly, recently chatted with one of her unbelieving friends, who said that she had no interest in Christianity, but would be willing to read through the whole Bible. Kimberly happily agreed to read through Scripture with her, but also suggested that they read through a book showing the overarching story of the Bible. Books like *The Drama of Scripture* and Vaughan Roberts' *God's Big Picture* are among the many that do this. For kids (but also for adults!), we also recommend Sally

Lloyd-Jones' book *The Jesus Storybook Bible*.[13] Concerning *discipleship*, seeing how themes develop across the biblical narrative and how they find their apex in Christ leads Christians to worship and ongoing transformation.

God is the ultimate storyteller, and there's no story like the story of salvation found in Holy Scripture. We should read with a magnifying glass (studying the details of a particular passage) and read with a wide-angle lens (considering the passage in view of the larger story).[14] This story leads us to faith in our Messiah, making us people of hope and joy. It's the story we need to be able to tell and retell to this broken world.

The work of gospelizing people

Jesus' view of the Bible was passed down to the apostles, as is evidenced in various places. For instance, Paul bookends his letter to the Romans with statements about the Old Testament and the Messiah (Rom. 1:1b–3; 16:25–27). In his opening words, he shows us how the gospel has its foundations in the Old Testament, declaring that the gospel is God's good news, promised in the Old Testament, centered on Jesus, designed to bring all peoples to the obedience of faith for the sake of Christ's name, and transforming everyone who believes (Rom. 1:1–3). Paul then spends many chapters articulating the gospel to *Christians* before getting to the more practical section of Romans 12–15.

Why does Paul spend so much time on the gospel? It is because the good news is not just about entry into heaven; it also shapes gospel-centered community and drives gospel-centered mission—very important subjects in this letter. In order to shape a community of both Jews and Gentiles, and have them support his ongoing mission to Spain, Paul spends a lot of time articulating the gospel. In his Romans commentary, New Testament scholar Mike Bird says that Paul is "gospelizing" the believers in Rome.[15] That is, Paul wants every aspect of their lives to be shaped and empowered by the gospel. Likewise, theologically driven church planters and leaders are committed to seeing every aspect of believers' lives shaped and empowered by the gospel.

There are at least five reasons why believers and churches should follow Paul's example and keep the gospel front and center.

The gospel changes lives

God loves to save sinners—and he does so when the gospel is announced to unbelievers. God loves to sanctify his people—and he does this as the gospel is applied to believers. We used to hear the phrase "life change" a lot in church circles, but how are lives changed? Lives are changed by the Life-Changer, Jesus Christ. To see lives changed, we need to keep the Life-Changer at the heart of everything.

The gospel leads us to worship

The good news changes us from the inside out. When affections change, everything changes. If a person loves Jesus deeply, it will change his or her behavior dramatically. Paul's theology regularly leads him to doxology (cf. Rom. 8:31–39; 11:33–36).

The gospel lifts us from despair

Sin, suffering, and death cause believers to despair. Much of ministry involves counseling those in despair. The gospel lifts us from dark nights of the soul by reminding the saints that God's verdict has already been pronounced over them; that though they're suffering, they're still in the grip of the Father's grace; and that even death can't separate them from the love of Christ.

The gospel unites diverse believers in community

As already noted, Paul is applying his theology in Romans to build a unified people who are quite diverse, as he does elsewhere (cf. Eph. 2:11–22). Real unity is built as we center on the gospel, and a lot of church fights wouldn't happen if we majored on the gospel rather than on preferences.

The gospel fuels our mission

It seems that many don't have a passion for the nations precisely because they don't have a gospel worth preaching. When we really marinate on the gospel's necessity and glory, we will want to commend it to the world. That's why it's no surprise where Paul goes at the end of Romans. In chapter 15, you discover that Romans is a missionary support letter! Paul wants to go to Spain with the gospel. Scholars such as Tom Schreiner have suggested that Paul could have been sixty years old at the time of writing. Though sixty, he wants to get the gospel where Jesus is neither named nor known! That's what the gospel does: it fuels our lives. You commend what you cherish, so as people cherish the gospel, they will naturally and instinctively want to commend Christ to the world.

Conclusion

Christianity is not the only religion in the world to have missionaries and preachers. What makes our mission and our proclamation unique is what we declare—namely, the gospel. This is why theological clarity matters. Faithful church planters around the world declare the good news concerning Jesus Christ to a world in darkness. Christ is central in Scripture, and history is moving to the day of Christ Jesus. Given these truths, it is imperative that church planters and ministry leaders stay focused on declaring Jesus as Lord to everyone worldwide, and on nurturing new believers with the word of Christ.

Reflection questions

1. Why does theological clarity matter when planting churches? Where might you run amuck without doctrinal precision and gospel centrality?

2. We need clarity on what we are starting. What is a local church? How do you form a church that grows in health and maturity?

3. What do you believe regarding church membership? Is it biblical? How would you seek to establish meaningful membership in the life of a new church?

4. How would you use the gospel in discipling a believer who is apathetic toward the church, drowning in marital conflict, raising rebellious children, addicted to pornography, *or* struggling with depression?

3

Conviction and Commendation

Adam Muhtaseb, my friend and fellow Acts 29 planter/ pastor, explained his conversion by saying, "When Islam choked me with 'Do, do, do,' Jesus said 'It's already done,' and captured my heart. That's how a Muslim kid eventually became a Christian church planter in one of America's most unreached cities."[16] Between his glorious conversion and his planting of Redemption City Church in Baltimore, Adam was part of our church, and I had the privilege of watching him mature and develop. In addition to having a robust gospel-centered theology, Adam had two things all church planters need: (1) a personal conviction to plant a church, and (2) a willingness to be patient until his elders confirmed that he was ready.

In fact, Adam had first been urged to plant a church immediately after doing some fruitful college ministry in Maryland. However, he sensed that he needed to learn more, be commended by mature leaders, and be sent out from a healthy, local church. So he came to be with us in

North Carolina for a season. I have had a front-row seat of watching this process, and now celebrate the impact he and his church are making in a hard city.

Conviction and *commendation* bring together the inward desire to start a church along with outside affirmation from other leaders. Conviction speaks to one's inner calling, passion, decisiveness, and willingness to sacrifice for the mission. Commendation speaks to the need for others to recognize and affirm the planter's gifts and maturity required for the work.

Conviction

In Romans 15:14–33, the apostle Paul describes his calling, past travels, and future plans for ministry. As he does, he says something significant regarding this idea of conviction, or as he calls it, *"ambition"* (Rom. 15:20). We get a glimpse inside the heart of the greatest missionary and church planter ever as he writes, "I make it my ambition to preach the gospel, not where Christ has already been named, lest I build on someone else's foundation, but as it is written, 'Those who have never been told of him will see, and those who have never heard will understand'" (Rom. 15:20–21). The work of preaching Christ where he was neither named nor known consumed the apostle Paul.

Antioch had been Paul's home base and sending church (Acts 13), but now he wants to go to Spain, and he wants the church in Rome to be the new Antioch, supporting his work in pioneer regions. Paul was passionate about this pioneering work of preaching Christ to unreached peoples and establishing new churches. Like modern-day church planters, his burning conviction to do this work made him willing to make great sacrifices.

A holy ambition

John Piper describes Paul's desire as being a "holy ambition" and that all Christians should have some kind of holy ambition.[17] While not everyone will share Paul's ambition to do pioneer evangelism and church planting, all Christians should be driven by the Great Commission and God's glory.

Not every aspiring church leader will go into church planting. Some will actually build on someone else's foundation (cf. 1 Cor. 3:5–11), leading established churches. This is a good thing. We certainly need faithful pastors to step into existing local churches and lead faithfully. But some ministers will have a desire similar to Paul's, eager to start from scratch in underserved and unreached areas. They will long to bring the gospel to hard places and see new churches started. This holy ambition drives their work.

Paul's *passion* inspires us to "fan into flame" the gifts God has given us (2 Tim. 1:6). His example of passion underscored an important reminder: people that make a tremendous gospel impact in the world are not always the most gifted; they are simply those most devoted to the cause. The secret to faithful church planting is not mastering a set of techniques and methods, but being mastered by theological, spiritual, and missional convictions.

Further, observe that Paul's ambition wasn't a personal agenda, but one driven by *Scripture*. In Romans 5:21, he quotes Isaiah 52:15. This shows that he is driven by the biblical expectation that the nations will be greatly amazed by the Suffering Servant. Paul longs to preach to people who had not been "told" or had ever "heard" about the good news, being encouraged by the expectation that many would hear and embrace Jesus. Church planters also go into the world with confidence that God has a people for himself, and that as the gospel is proclaimed, many will respond in faith (cf. Acts 18:10).

Strikingly, Paul doesn't mention a personal or experiential calling here. He mentions Scripture as his driving motivation. I am not discounting this kind of personal calling (Paul alludes to his in places like Acts 26:12–18), but just pointing out that Paul's consuming ambition is found in a text (Isa. 52:13–15ff). Piper comments:

When Jesus called Paul on the Damascus road to take the gospel to the Gentiles who had never heard, Paul went to the Old Testament and looked for a confirmation and explanation of this calling to see how it fit into God's overall plan. And he found it. And for our sake he speaks this way. He doesn't just refer to his experience on the Damascus road, which we will never have. He refers to God's written word that we do have. And he roots his ambition there.[18]

Aspiring church planters need to meditate on Scripture day and night to get direction, to deepen their theological and missional convictions, and to embolden them for the work.

As I mentioned in the last chapter, Tom Schreiner states that Paul would have been about sixty years old when stating this holy ambition![19] This vision of a sixty-year-old, war-torn apostle desiring to go to Spain, to reach unreached people groups and start new churches, is truly inspiring. His conviction was born out of Scripture, likely with deep reflection on Isaiah's vision of the coastlands hearing the good news (cf. Isa. 11:11; 41:1; 42:4, 10; 49:1; 51:5; 60:9; 66:19–20).

It is this holy ambition, this consuming gospel conviction, that will keep you from fizzling out or giving up. Ministry is not for the faint of heart, and church planting is laborious. If one ever envisions church planting as glamorous, they only need to read about Paul's afflictions, noted in various places (cf. 2 Cor. 6:3–10; 11:23b–28). He traveled hundreds and hundreds of miles, and was not doing so in a nice Hummer with air-conditioning. Advancing the gospel always requires sacrifice, and church planting will bring with it a host of challenges. You will face spiritual opposition (2 Cor. 4:3–4). You may even face violent opposition from people. You will be tempted to grow discouraged or anxious. You will have to deal with conflict among your people. There will be long days of doing all sorts of things (meetings, emails, fundraising, sermon prep, counseling, writing, prayer, and more). We go in the Lord's strength (2 Tim. 2:1;

Eph. 6:10), compelled by a holy ambition to make Christ known and to see churches planted.

Heart questions

Potential church planters need to wrestle with important heart questions like: "Do I have an intense, all-absorbing desire for this work?" "Am I willing to make hard sacrifices for this mission?" The work is simply too demanding and too important not to have a deep sense of calling and conviction.

Trying to discern whether or not one should plant a new church often becomes clearer over time. When I went to seminary, I knew I wanted to preach and do ministry, but I wasn't exactly sure what this would look like. I loved evangelistic preaching and doing student ministry, but over time, church planting became a passionate desire. Interestingly, a class on church administration impacted me. In this class, we studied all kinds of things related to the church. I had never thought about childcare check-in, parking lot workers, deacon ministry, hospital visitation, pastoral rhythms, small-group methods, and many other practical matters. Reflecting on Romans 15:20 and these course lectures, I began asking, "What would it look like if I started a church, building on no one else's foundation?" I didn't immediately plant a church then, but this burning desire never left me. My wife and I discussed church planting regularly until we eventually planted Imago Dei ten years ago.

You don't go into church planting because you think it's cool, to prove something to others, or to boost your ego. Faithful church planters are driven by spiritual convictions that have been born out of deep thought and prayer, and a strong sense of the Lord's providential guidance.

Commendation

Church planters should never operate as lone rangers. While it is good and right to have an inward drawing to plant a church, this should be accompanied by the external confirmation of others. What should they be able to observe? I'll mention four characteristics.

Maturity

The apostle warns about giving spiritual leadership to "a recent convert" (1 Tim. 3:6) and to not "be hasty in the laying on of hands" (5:22). Maturity is mandatory for ministry leadership (2 Tim. 2:22–26; 3:10–11). Mature leaders in the congregation have a responsibility to identify and affirm new mature leaders (Tit. 1:5–9).

In Acts 16, we read of Paul taking Timothy with him. Luke tells us that Timothy was "well spoken of by the brothers" (Acts 16:2). Timothy obviously displayed a sense of maturity, and the saints in Lystra and Iconium would have approved of the young man accompanying Paul. We also see this kind of confirmation when Paul speaks of the elders laying their hands on Timothy (1 Tim. 4:14). There was spiritual affirmation and approval.

Desire

Godly people should also see in a potential planter a real desire for kingdom work. They should observe a hunger for Scripture. They should detect humility and an enjoyment of ministry. They should see a passion and a willingness to sacrifice for the mission. Close friends and one's spouse (if married) should be able to attest to these things as well. If married, it's critical that the planter's wife also shares a passion for gospel ministry and church planting.

Speaking about entering the ministry in general, Charles Spurgeon said,

> "Do not enter the ministry if you can help it," was the deeply sage advice of a divine to one who sought his judgment. If any student in this room could be a newspaper editor, or a grocer, or a farmer, or a doctor, or a lawyer, or a senator, or a king, in the name of heaven and earth let him go his way.[20]

Indeed, the call to ministry involves great passion. Paul says, "If anyone *aspires* to the office of overseer, he *desires* a noble task" (1 Tim. 3:1, my emphasis). When Paul spoke about preaching, he also displayed this passion: "For if I preach the gospel, that gives me no ground for boasting. For necessity is laid upon me. Woe to me if I do not preach the gospel!" (1 Cor. 9:16). This kind of passion— for gospel ministry in general and church planting in particular—should be something other mature Christians see in aspiring planters.

Abilities

Church planters also need to display certain gifts. They should be able to minister the Word faithfully and effectively (1 Tim. 3:2). They should be good at engaging unbelievers. They should be able to gather a team and lead others spiritually. They should show the ability to make the most of gospel opportunities with the gifts God has given them. Tim Keller comments on the importance of one's skills and abilities, and the value of experienced leaders speaking into the potential planter's life:

> *The success in starting a new church is largely determined by who is selected as the church planter. To establish a new church requires of the church planter distinct gifts, skills and experiences in ministry often not found in a normal pastor. Though there are many similarities in these two roles, the church planter must thrive in outreach ministry and in developing and empowering new leaders. Although self-evaluation is important in understanding one's gifts and call, much can be learned by inviting the objective evaluation of experienced church planters.*[21]

Going through a church-planting assessment is one way we take this external confirmation seriously. At our church, the pastors assess our planters, and we ask several people about their maturity and gifts. In Acts 29, we also use a thorough assessment process for potential church planters who want to belong to our network. While this assessment can be a bit painful because it opens one up to critique, it's actually a wonderful blessing. It serves to bring awareness to one's blind spots, it highlights areas for needed growth, and it can prevent many problems in the future (like burnout, marital issues, theological errors, or financial problems). The assessment process is like a high-level discipleship process. Walking through such a process will bring a heightened sense of confidence for the work ahead once the process is completed.

Fruitfulness

Mature leaders should see that others have been blessed by the potential planter's ministry in some particular way. That is, when he has had the opportunity to teach or preach, his ministry had a gospel impact. They see that he's been able to disciple others into maturity. They see that he has engaged lost people well. Perhaps they have observed his ability to lead a small group faithfully. If a potential planter has not made any disciples or displayed any ministry fruitfulness, then it begs the question about his ability to plant a church and lead a group of people on mission.

One of the tasks of planters/pastors is to always be on the lookout for future leaders and planters. In addition to having a "to-do list," one pastor said we should also have a "to-be list." We should always be looking for faithful, budding leaders who display maturity, passion, gifting, and fruitfulness. Identifying them, investing in them, and sending them out on mission is a vitally important aspect of pastoral leadership.

Conclusion

Church planters are driven by deep, personal convictions for the work, born out of Scripture, deep thought, and prayer. Their passion for planting a new church means they're willing to work hard and make sacrifices. But they also recognize the need for others to commend them for the work, so they should not be hasty in the process. Mature leaders should see their holy ambition, spiritual maturity, and abilities to lead a new church, and fruitfulness in the aspiring planter's present ministry. To start more healthy, multiplying churches, church leaders need to give serious investment to aspiring planters, emphasizing both this inner conviction and external commendation.

Reflection questions

1. Consider for a moment these issues: leadership, context, and timing. Why do you think God might be leading you to plant a church? Why you? Why there? Why now?

2. What passages of Scripture has God used to cultivate within you a desire for the work of church planting?

3. What sacrifices are you willing to make to see a church formed? What sacrifices are you unwilling to make?

4. Who can speak to your maturity as a leader, your desire for this work, the gifts God has given you, and your fruitfulness in ministry? How have they affirmed you thus far?

4

A Healthy Marriage

You obviously don't have to be married to be a church planter or be on a church-planting team. After all, the greatest church planter ever, the apostle Paul, wasn't married! And I could list many other faithful planters/ pastors who were or are single (Charles Simeon, John Stott, Vaughan Roberts, Hunter Beaumont, and others). In fact, there are some great advantages in not being married, as Paul describes in 1 Corinthians 7. However, many church planters are married, and this subject is significant for a number of reasons, like the fact that faithfulness in marriage is a qualification for a pastor (cf. 1 Tim. 3:2). If marriages are not healthy, then many problems will arise, some of which can be devastating.

Let's consider: (1) the foundation for marriage, (2) the glory of marriage, and (3) the practice of marriage.

The foundation for marriage

The first place we turn on this subject is the opening chapters of Genesis. Marriage is God's idea (cf. Mat. 19:4–10). In the beginning, God creates everything. He is God over it all. But there was one thing that wasn't good: an alone man, Adam.

So God decides to create a suitable "helper" for him (Gen. 2:18). Genesis 1:27 tells us that God created "man in his own image," equal in value and dignity, as "male and female." The creation of Eve led to the first union between man and woman—a holy one-flesh union and a complementary relationship (cf. Eph. 5:22–33). John Stott provides a helpful and concise definition: "Marriage is an exclusive heterosexual covenant between one man and one woman, ordained and sealed by God, preceded by the leaving of parents, consummated in sexual union, issuing in a permanently supportive partnership, and normally crowned with the gift of children."[22] Indeed, there are many important truths to consider on this subject, but let's begin by considering four purposes of this covenantal relationship.

Marriage is for partnership

At the foundation of a healthy marriage is companionship (cf. Prov. 2:17). The author of Song of Solomon declared, "This is my beloved and this is my friend" (5:16b). Initially, Adam had animals, but he didn't have a wife! One of the great gifts in marriage is companionship.

My wife and I met working at a Christian youth camp (a stereotypical story, I know!) and were married a few years later. We have only known each other in the context of doing ministry together, and this has been a tremendous blessing. She truly is my "dear companion" and my partner in ministry. Show me a faithful church planter who is bearing much fruit, and more times than not, you will hear him testify to how his bride is laboring side by side with him. She may not be doing the same things other pastors' wives are doing, but she's there as his companion in life and ministry.

If you are single and in ministry, then we should remember that the church is God's gift to everyone for deep community. I have heard from several single pastors that the church has provided such rich friendship and gospel partnership through the years.

Marriage is for procreation

Procreation is not the only purpose of marriage, and it's not necessary for a planter to have children, but one of the divine purposes of marriage is to "be fruitful and multiply" (Gen. 1:28). Our church is really good at this!

The church views children as wonderful gifts from God (cf. Ps .127–128). One of the blessings of community is investing in and caring for one another's children.

Marriage is for pleasure

Marriage is not only a gift, but is romance. While many may blush at this idea of talking about the goodness of sex within marriage, it shouldn't be ignored (1 Cor. 7:1–5). To be sure, there are other pleasures in marriage, but this has to be at the top of the list (cf. Heb. 13:4). The writer of Proverbs teaches men to find their pleasure in the wife of their youth (Prov. 5:18–20). Further, the writer of Song of

Solomon speaks in vivid terms about enjoying each other: "Let him kiss me with the kisses of his mouth! For your love is better than wine" (1:2), to quote one of the more modest lines in the book!

If you are married and in ministry, it is important to cultivate romance in your marriage. For a good marriage is not only one that you endure but one that you enjoy. Marriages that contain frequent intimate experiences do a number of things, like keep the tempter away (1 Cor. 7:5b). Satan would love to keep married couples away from each other.

Marriage is a picture

Marriage pictures the covenant-keeping love of Christ for his bride, the church (cf. Eph. 5:22–33). This fact should constantly amaze us. After citing Genesis 2:24, Paul writes, "This mystery is profound, and I am saying that it refers to Christ and the church" (Eph. 5:32). Nowhere else in the world do people have such a view of marriage as those who embrace this biblical vision.

The point of marriage is ultimately not the relationship between husband and wife but that between Christ and his church. Borrowing a line I heard, I've often quipped, "Kimberly and I have a perfect marriage. It's just not with each other! It's with Christ." While we do have a wonderful marriage, for which I give God praise, our marriage is not ultimate. Neither is yours, Christian, if you're married. Since you are united to Christ, and because of the temporary nature of marriage, there's actually freedom in knowing you don't have to idolize marriage. Even if you have a great marriage, it's a shadow of the glorious union to come. And if some things aren't right in your marriage, it's okay to admit that right now and to begin to seek help, change, and grow.

The glory of marriage

The Bible begins and ends with a wedding (Gen. 2:18ff; Rev. 19:6ff). If that weren't significant enough, Jesus' first miracle was at a wedding. Like most ideas in Scripture, first things are important things.

The story of Jesus turning water into wine at a wedding (John 2:1–11) reveals several important truths, including the fact that John says this miracle is a "sign" (2:11). If you wanted to change the world and could perform miracles, why choose this one to be your first? Don't get me wrong, it's wonderful! Jesus takes a ruinous situation and turns it into a party. (I love that Jesus performed his first miracle at a wedding and not at a dirge!) But I don't think one would say this is more fascinating than walking on water? This miracle was a quiet miracle, and it wasn't a life-or-death situation. It's basically a social crisis. So why does Jesus do this one?

By calling this miracle a "sign," John is pointing to the greater story that's being told here. Not only has Jesus come to give joy and not take it, but Jesus' first miracle is a foretaste of the greater wedding, a greater feast, a greater party to come.

If you are a single minister or a married one, recognize that we all stand in awe of this reality. This is where we want to lead everyone to: Jesus Christ, the Lord of the Feast. In the Old Testament, the Messiah was associated with a feast (Jer. 31:12; Amos 9:13–14; Isa. 25:6; Luke 14:12ff). In this story in John 2, Jesus has his wedding on his mind. Jesus would soon lay down his life for his bride. He provides the greatest of all unions and the best of joys. In Scripture, Jesus relates to his people in various relationships, like as a shepherd to sheep and as a king to a servant, but the best of all is as a groom to his bride.

This groom-bride relationship tells us essential truths not only about Jesus but also about us. It tells us that we are made for such a relationship. It tells us that we long to be received and embraced, known and loved. If you are in Christ, then know that he loves you beyond any love that a man may have for a woman or vice versa. There is no union like the union of Christ to his church. We can take every need to him. We rest in his love. We find satisfaction in him, for in Jesus, the wine never runs out.

God did not create the world to show off the laws of physics or mathematics or unleash the laws of ethics of chemistry. He created the world to redeem a bride. We await the fullness of our union with Christ when he returns. In the meantime, we proclaim this message to a world in need of this relationship.

The practice of marriage

Over the past few years, I've learned of some well-known church leaders who were removed from ministry due to unfaithfulness in marriage. Interestingly, the men I have in mind were known for having morning devotional time and practicing various spiritual gifts. However, their marriages weren't healthy, and each of these men was unfaithful to his wife. I have since grown to see how one can envision personal holiness in a privatized way while neglecting relational holiness. Married men, the pursuit of your wife and the cultivation of a faithful and joyful marriage must be at the heart of your pursuit of holiness. If not, then you are in a walking disaster zone.

In a non-exhaustive way, allow me to lay out eight marks of a faithful and joyful marriage, using the acronym FAITHFUL.

F – Friendship

If you are in a covenant marriage, then let me encourage you to have fun together! My bride goes to baseball games with me; I go to musicals with her. I make her pour-over coffee in the morning. We have date nights. I love being married! Underneath this friendship is that which is foundational in any relationship: trust. The writer of Proverbs 31 speaks of an excellent wife, saying, "The heart of her husband trusts her" (31:11a). In a good marriage, each spouse trusts the other, which is vital for not only remaining faithful to each other in this covenantal relationship, but also for maintaining a joyous friendship. The writer of the book of Ecclesiastes, having talked about how hard life is, bursts out with several things to enjoy in this life. He includes bread, wine, white garments, and oil

(9:7–8). Before adding one's toil to this list, he says, "Enjoy life with the wife whom you love" (9:9a).

A – Affection

Fondness and warmth come through nearness to each other and personal touch and interaction with each other. We must avoid harshness (Col. 3:19) and strive after deep affection for one another. Over time, it's possible for love to grow cold if each spouse turns inward or selfish. The goal is not to co-exist but to practice empathy, kindness, and comfort for one another.

I – Intimacy

Interestingly, in Hebrews 13, the author puts money and marriage side by side as important areas in which to please God (13:4–5). It's a great reminder that many of our battles will come in the realm of sex and money. If you're married, consider ways to ensure not only financial integrity but also romantic intimacy. How many ministers have fallen in one of these two areas!

T – Teamwork

Church planters, if you're married and in ministry, find ways for your wife to flourish in ministry with you. Avoid compartmentalizing your life so much that there's a great divide between ministry life and family life. While I realize you need special alone time with your bride, seek to do ministry with your wife.

H – Honor

We find the call to honor one another in Scripture. Paul writes, "However, let each one of you love his wife as himself, and let the wife see that she *respects* her husband" (Eph. 5:33, my emphasis). Peter writes, "Likewise, husbands live with your wives in an understanding way, showing honor to the woman as the weaker vessel" (1 Pet. 3:7a). Find ways to honor your spouse regularly. Avoid disrespecting each other in verbal or non-verbal ways. Seek to honor each other in front of others. Elsewhere, Paul says, "Outdo one another in showing honor" (Rom. 12:10b). While he is speaking about the Christian community in general here, his admonition is a good goal for a marriage

F – Forgiveness

A faithful marriage doesn't mean a perfect marriage. Spouses will fail each other and sin against one another. When that happens, we have the great opportunity to repent and seek forgiveness, and to extend forgiveness. Forgiven people forgive people. Therefore, each spouse should reflect deeply on God's forgiveness in order to be compelled to reflect his forgiveness to the other (cf. Eph. 4:32). The psalmist said, "If you, O Lord, should mark iniquities, O Lord, who could stand? But with you there is forgiveness, that you may be feared" (Ps. 130:3–4). May we who have been forgiven, more than we even realize, seek to display God's mercy to others, especially our spouses.

U – Understanding

While each spouse needs to seek to understand each other, Peter applies this point particularly to husbands, whom he urges to live with their wife in an "understanding way" (1 Pet. 3:7). This implies trying to see things through her eyes. It means paying attention to her. It means allowing her to talk. It means learning what she likes and what she doesn't, and knowing her fears and her cares. Seek to know how she is doing physically, emotionally, spiritually, and relationally. To do all this, you must communicate! A major obstacle to a healthy marriage is the lack of communication, which can lead to a lack of understanding and care.

L – Labor

To love someone is to sacrifice for them. This means sacrificing time, schedules, and, sometimes, good ambitions. A healthy marriage takes work. But this service is not a burden when it is motivated by love! Recall how Jacob labored seven years for Rachel, but the writer of Genesis says, "they seemed to him but a few days because of the love he had for her" (29:20). The same is true for our labor for Christ; the labor comes easy when motivated by love for the Savior.

May the Lord give those of you who are married a marathon marriage. May your marriage bring you great joy, may it bring God glory, and may it point others to the ultimate union of Christ and his bride.

Conclusion

If you are married and either in ministry or aspiring to ministry, then you need to give attention to your marriage. If not, there will be disastrous results, and you will miss out on other joyous blessings. Let us never forget that our marriages are designed to reflect Christ's love for the church. So let each of us care for our spouses in a way that reflects this ultimate union by faithfully following the biblical description of a godly and flourishing marital relationship.

Reflection questions

1. How have you experienced the grace of God in your marriage so far in navigating together through sin and suffering from without and within?

2. How do you think your wife would describe your care and spiritual leadership toward her and your family (as it relates to time, money, parenting, affection, intimacy, and so on)?

3. What are your three greatest strengths and weaknesses as a husband and a father?

4. How do you and your wife team with one another in life and ministry? Provide practical examples of how you have done this both well and poorly throughout your marriage.

Here are some additional questions for the wife of a prospective church planter:

1. Do you believe your husband possesses the spiritual, moral, and emotional maturity necessary to serve as a pastor-planter? Are there any issues in your husband's life, your life, or your family's life that might make it wise for your husband *not* to be a pastor-planter at this time?

2. How convinced are you that God is leading your family to be part of planting a church?

3. What sacrifices are you willing to make to see this come to fruition? What sacrifices are you unwilling to make?

4. In what ways do you personally hope to contribute to this missional endeavor? What aspects of what may be expected of you would you want to avoid?

5

Healthy Relationships

Prior to my first semester of seminary, I devoured the seminary catalog. I was so eager to begin my studies. But as I surveyed the programs and required courses for my degree, one class kind of puzzled me: interpersonal relationship skills. Why would a future pastor or ministry leader need this course? I mean, biblical studies and theology made sense, but this class seemed unnecessary. However, the course was the result of research on why the graduates had a hard time in the local church. This wasn't due to their theology or preaching skills; it was due to their failure to cultivate and maintain healthy relationships.

So, in my first semester, I would go to a course on expository preaching at 8 a.m., and then I studied interpersonal relationship skills at 9 a.m. Looking back, I see this as illustrative of ministry. Pastors and church leaders must rightly handle the Word of truth (cf., 2 Tim 2:15; 1 Tim 3:2; 4:16), but we must also remember that pastoral ministry is people-focused. We must lead people humbly (cf. 1 Pet. 5:1–5), love people genuinely (cf. 1 Tim. 4:12; 2 Tim. 4:22), deal with conflict peaceably (cf. Matt. 5:9; Rom. 14:19), deal with critics gently (2 Tim. 2:25), and love outsiders warmly (1 Tim. 3:7; Tit. 1:8). Further, Paul says overseers (if they are married) must love their wives faithfully (1 Tim. 3:2), and they must manage their own households well (1 Tim. 3:4–5; Tit. 1:6). Relationships matter—in the home, in the church, and among the outside world.

The call to honor Christ in our relationships by following the teaching of Scripture is the calling for all Christians—whether or not one is in vocational ministry. While there are some differences in how pastors relate to parishioners, this competency is primarily about basic discipleship principles for all believers. The unique challenge for pastors and ministry leaders is to set the believers *an example* in this area (1 Tim. 4:12).

Gospel-driven relationships

One could look to a number of texts to think about healthy relationships, but a go-to passage for me is Romans 12:9–21.

Romans 12:1 marks a new section in the letter to the Romans. Believers are exhorted to live in view of God's "mercies" (12:1)—the glorious gospel that we read about in Romans 1–11. Christians are to offer our bodies as "a living sacrifice" to God (Rom. 12:1) and to be transformed through the renewal of our minds (12:2). One of the primary ways Romans 12:1–2 will be lived out is by the Christian giving himself or herself to the church, through the use of their spiritual gifts

(12:3–8), and through gospel-centered acts of love in their relationships (12:9–16).

Paul is dealing in the book of Romans with a conflict between Jews and Gentiles (see 14:1ff). The church had become fractured along ethnic lines. The leadership was mainly Gentile. The meetings were not in synagogues but in house churches. The Jewish believers would have found many of the Gentile cultural practices offensive. All of this gives rise to Paul's glorious multi-ethnic vision for the people of God. All of this lies behind the entire letter.

Paul argues that unity between Jews and Gentiles could only be established in the gospel (not in preferences and opinions). So Paul spends chapter after chapter explaining the gospel before getting to chapter 12, where he will apply it in relationships. He shows us how we are to love, avoid division, and experience loving harmony in the church.

Romans 1–11 has some sections that are difficult to understand. Romans 12:9–21 is not that difficult to understand, but it's difficult to live! That's because it's about relationships.

I'm reminded of the cartoon where Linus quips, "I love mankind; it's people I can't stand." It's easy to love the idea of the church, but quite another thing to love real people in the church. This is why we need the regular renewal of our minds! Renewed minds lead to new attitudes, relationships, and practices that are not conformed to this world. It's easy to do the opposite of these instructions and be conformed to the world's mindset. Romans 12 is calling us to something beautifully different. We need hearts that are saturated in grace to live these instructions out. We need to keep the gospel central to do this—especially in these divided days in which we live.

The fact is that if these verses were lived out faithfully, it would radically change our world. It changed the first-century, Greco-Roman world as the church lived as a counter-culture—a little outpost of the kingdom of God. They lived out these instructions in a hierarchal culture and in an honor and shame culture. In doing so, they said to the world, "You want to know what the kingdom is like—here's a glimpse. It's not perfect, but it's a glimpse." In God's kingdom, there's love and honor, passion and perseverance, generosity and hospitality, rejoicing and weeping, harmony and humility, and goodness and peacemaking.

Pursuing and maintaining gospel-centered relationships

What Paul urges the Romans to do is essentially to allow the gospel to shape and empower their relationships with others. We can observe them in six categories.

Love and honor (12:9–10)

Paul says, "Let love be genuine" (12:9a), which serves as a kind of header over the whole section. Real love is sincere. It's not fake. There's no deception or play-acting. Christian love is never to be a guise for ulterior motives. As pastors, we're called to genuinely love the people in our care, and not see them as "numbers" or as a means to some end. As undershepherds of the Chief Shepherd, we love the sheep. We follow Jesus' example in John 13.

Further, genuine love means that we're quick to forgive and quick to apologize. It means that we avoid partiality and love each member in our care. It means we know our people, and we pay attention to their cares and needs (cf. Phil. 2:20). It means we display warmth and welcome.

Paul helps us avoid a misunderstanding of love when he says, "Abhor what is evil; hold fast to what is good" (Rom. 12:9b). Love doesn't allow evil to persist in the name of "love." Love actually hates certain things. We are to pursue holy love. Love is not genuine when it leads a person to do something evil, allows a person to do evil, or when it avoids addressing evil. Love knows the difference between right and wrong (cf. 1 Cor. 13:6). Good parents don't allow their kids to do just anything in the name of love, and good pastors will also address evil as an act of love for the church fellowship.

Further, this genuine love is marked by "brotherly affection" (Rom. 12:10a). Christians should seek to cultivate tenderness, warmth, and affection. In his *Lectures to My Students*, pastor Charles Spurgeon exhorted his students to cultivate this kind of heart, saying:

> *I love a minister whose face invites me to make him my friend ... on whose doorstep you read "Welcome," not "Beware of Dog." ... Give me the man around whom the children come. ... An individual who doesn't have*

*a friendly, cheerful manner about him had better be an
undertaker, and bury the dead, for he will never succeed
in influencing the living. ... A man must have a great heart
if he is to have a great congregation. ... When a man has
a large, loving heart, men go to him as ships to a haven. ...
Such a man is hearty in private as well as in public.*[23]

May God make us these kinds of leaders!

Regarding honor, Paul says to the church, "Outdo one
another in showing honor" (Rom. 12:10b). This was a
radical command in the first-century, hierarchical world
(cf. Rom. 12:17; 13:7; 1 Pet. 2:17). I'm always struck by the
kind of respect Paul conveyed as he preached the gospel to
Felix and Agrippa at the end of Acts. It is also striking how
Paul honors faithful servants in the church throughout his
letters (cf. Rom. 16:1–16). As planters and ministry leaders,
look for ways to honor faithful servants in the church.

Passion and perseverance (12:11–12)

The next verse drips with passion: "Do not be slothful in
zeal, be fervent in spirit, serve the Lord" (12:11). Christian
love is not cold or indifferent! In the previous passage,
Paul singled out leaders saying that those with the gift of
leadership must lead "with zeal" (12:8). That is, we are
to be set on fire by the Spirit (12:11), who empowers our
leadership, and keep in constant view the focus of our
ministry: serving the Lord. Jesus is the object of our zeal.
A passion for Christ and a compassion for his people are
at the heart of faithful ministry.

This verse hangs over my bed in my home: "Rejoice in hope, be patient in tribulation, be constant in prayer" (12:12). The theme of perseverance ties these three phrases together.

Life and ministry are hard, but we can derive hope and joy in Christ, and we can find strength through prayer. How do we endure "tribulation" without murmuring and self-pity? By applying the other two parts of the verse: *rejoicing and praying*. If a ministry leader is not rejoicing and praying personally, then that leader won't be persevering faithfully.

Generosity and hospitality (12:13)

Here are two practical ways to love and pursue harmony: generosity and hospitality. Christian leaders are to set an example of generosity (cf. Acts 4:36–37; 20:35). And we must never be driven by greed (cf. 1 Tim. 6:5; 1 Pet. 5:2). Rather, we are to be cheerful givers, as we remember that our God is a giver (cf. Rom. 8:32).

Further, we are to welcome others as we have been welcomed by God in Christ (cf. Isa. 25:6–7; 55:1–3; Matt. 11:28; Luke 14:12–24; Rom. 15:7; Rev. 21:3). Peter urges Christians to do this without grumbling (1 Pet. 4:9). Here in Romans 12, Paul speaks of the intentionality of it: *pursue it*. For pastors, this is a qualification for ministry (cf. 1 Tim. 3:2). If one does not welcome others into their home, their church, and their lives, then that person doesn't belong in ministry. Interestingly, I have heard of potential pastors "preaching in view of a call," but I've never heard of them "practicing hospitality in view of a call." However, this practice is vital for pastoral ministry, for evangelism and mercy ministry, and for the work of church planting.

Certainly, church leaders must use wisdom in practicing hospitality, but this doesn't mean we should neglect it or minimize its importance. Instead, we should promote hospitality and set a good example of doing it.

Rejoicing and weeping (12:15)

I'll deal with Romans 12:14 in the sixth category, as it relates more to our relationship with our enemies. In verse 15, Paul says: "Rejoice with those who rejoice, weep with those who weep." All Christians are to come alongside their brothers and sisters in the highs and lows of life, with pastors setting the believers an example in this area. When one person succeeds, rejoice with them! And when they are hurting, weep with them.

Many Christian leaders have a ministry of *truth* but not a ministry of *tears*. Jesus displayed both. He brought people the words of life and he wept at Lazarus' tomb— even though he knew he was about to raise him to life. The Good Shepherd in John 10 demonstrated this pastoral care in John 11. He entered into the grief of his friends and wept with them (John 11:35). We, too, need an integrated ministry of both mind and heart, emotions and theology, tears and truth.

Harmony and humility (12:16)

Paul tells the Roman Christians, "Live in harmony with one another" (Rom. 12:16a). He later prays for such harmony (15:5). He wanted them to be of the same mind (Phil. 2:1–5). This unity reflected the nature of God and gave a powerful witness to the world. An ongoing challenge in pastoral ministry is helping brothers and sisters deal with conflict, hurt feelings, and misunderstanding. Harmony takes hard work. The kind of harmony we're after is not merely an absence of strife but the presence of unity (cf. Ps. 133).

To have harmony, humility must be present: "Do not be haughty, but associate with the lowly. Never be wise in your own sight" (Rom. 12:16b). This fact is taught elsewhere in the New Testament (Phil. 2:1–4). One of the signs of humility is associating with all kinds of people. As church leaders, we should constantly evaluate our own lives to ensure that we are pursuing humility, but we must also teach and lead in such a way that we're fostering humility in the church.

Goodness and peacemaking (12:14, 17–21)

In Romans 12:14, Paul reflects on the teaching of Jesus regarding our enemies (Matt. 5:44; Luke 6:28). Notice we're not simply to refrain from retaliating, or should we simply forgive our enemies; we're also to actively seek their good as we pray for God's blessing on them! This verse is particularly relevant for those in ministry because you will have many opportunities to apply this verse, for there are many adversaries out there.

In verses 17–21, Paul highlights more action steps regarding our relationship to our enemies, emphasizing non-retaliation and peacemaking. We're to seek to live honorably among everyone, to do everything we can to live peaceably with all, and to leave vengeance to God. He ends the section with a summary admonition: "Do not be overcome by evil, but overcome evil with good" (12:21). We must disciple and counsel our members in this area!

Of course, on a civil level, we need courts and law enforcement. Paul isn't teaching that you let abuse or violence go unchecked. The very next passage (Rom. 13:1–7) is about how the state has the right to bear the sword, how God has appointed government as the institution to carry out judgment on earth. As good citizens, we need to promote biblical justice now, but ultimately, we trust in the Lord's final judgment in the future.

Christians deal with their enemies by grace and goodness, not by vengeance and vitriol. We do this motivated by Christ's work for us on the cross in the past, and by our belief about the coming day in the future. At the cross, Christ loved his enemies. He has made sinners— former enemies—his friends (Rom. 5:10; Col. 1:20–23). He overcame our evil with his goodness. And one day, he will have the final word on all those who oppose him and his people. So we can focus now on blessing, not vengeance. We can be people of grace, peace, and honor until the final day.

Conclusion

Relationships matter in the Christian life, and church planters and ministry leaders are to set the believers an example in cultivating and maintaining Christ-honoring relationships. The gospel must be proclaimed by church leaders, but the gospel must also shape and empower our relationships with those inside and outside the church.

Reflection questions

1. How are you seeking to cultivate and maintain healthy relationships?

2. Who are some of the people with whom you have cultivated close relationships? How long have you known them and what do your conversations sound like?

3. How would you say your own practice of hospitality has built community around you?

4. How have you sought to lay your preferences aside and genuinely love others? Can you provide an example of this?

6

Godly Leadership

In a very real sense, every chapter in this book is about godly leadership, and there are a number of directions I could go discussing this topic. But what I would like to do is simply to draw your attention to 1 Peter 5, and to consider one of the dominant images for leading God's people: *the shepherd.*

> *So I exhort the elders among you, as a fellow elder and a witness of the sufferings of Christ, as well as a partaker in the glory that is going to be revealed: shepherd the flock of God that is among you, exercising oversight, not under compulsion, but willingly, as God would have you; not for shameful gain, but eagerly; not domineering over those in your charge, but being examples to the flock. And when the chief Shepherd appears, you will receive the unfading crown of glory. Likewise, you who are younger, be subject to the elders. Clothe yourselves, all of you, with humility toward one another, for "God opposes the proud but gives grace to the humble." (1 Pet. 5:1–5)*

The church flourishes under happy, holy, and humble shepherds. The church suffers under domineering, corrupt, and cowardly leaders. In a time in which we read of scandal after scandal, we need to show the world a different picture of leadership—one that reflects the ministry of the Good Shepherd, Jesus (John 10:1–18).

What is particularly striking about Peter's exhortation is that he focuses so much attention on the *heart* of pastoral leaders. He tells us why we should serve and why we should not. It's possible for ministry leaders to be theologically astute, have a bunch of degrees, have a magnetic personality, be able to cast vision clearly, and be able to create Christ-centered sermons but be driven by wrong motivations. The results of this will be disastrous. This is why I keep coming back to passages like this one. I don't want to be that guy. And most people who have failed in pastoral leadership didn't start out wanting to be that guy either.

Shepherd the flock of God

Church planters should not envision their work apart from doing the work of pastoring. Even in the early days of your core team gatherings, you will be doing pastoral work. Once the church is established, you will be doing more pastoral work. As the church grows, again, more pastoral work will be needed.

While it's good to know some practical leadership skills, and even have a working understanding of business principles, we should envision our work being, first and foremost, about shepherding people. The good news about shepherding is that we don't have to do it alone! Notice how Peter refers to himself as a "fellow elder" (1 Pet. 5:1). The plurality of elders is normative in the New Testament, and it is practically beneficial, as well (cf. Acts 11:30; 14:21–23; 15:2; 20:17ff; Tit. 1:5).

We encourage our planters to plant with another pastorally qualified person. Having other pastors with you will protect you from mistakes you would make as a lone pastor; it makes up for your deficiencies; it makes your job more enjoyable; it provides accountability and encouragement; it allows you to divide the shepherding responsibilities; and it's the best way to transition if a pastor departs.

Notice also that Peter calls himself a "fellow elder" even though he was one of the twelve and "a witness to the sufferings of Christ" (1 Pet. 5:1). He didn't distance himself or elevate himself from the other elders, but humbly took his position beside them.

One of the most overlooked words in this passage is the little word "So" (5:1) or "Therefore" (NASB). This word draws our attention back to the previous chapter, which is about suffering and persecution. Think how this famous passage about pastoral leadership is written in the context of being afflicted for the sake of the gospel. Peter may be connecting us back to 1 Peter 4:12–19 because often, in hostile settings, the pastors are the first to be persecuted. Or he may be saying that because opposition puts a strain on the community, the need for faithful leadership increases; that is, people need leadership more—not less—in difficult times. In either case, there's no room for self-pity in ministry leadership. We signed up for hardship. Pastors in various places worldwide understand that you enter the ministry with your eyes wide open to the possibility of persecution. Let us never forget this, and let us be prepared to shepherd well when hard times come.

Peter underlines the responsibility of pastors as being to "shepherd the flock of God that is among you, exercising oversight" (5:2). The idea of being a shepherd is a rich biblical theme, with many examples to consider (for example, Gen. 48:15; Ex. 3:1; Ps. 23; 77:20; 78:52, 72; Isa. 40:11; Jer. 23; Ezek. 34; Mic. 5:2, 4; Matt. 9:36). However, Jesus is the Good Shepherd (John 10:1–18), the Great Shepherd (Heb. 13:20), and the Chief Shepherd (1 Pet. 5:4). In his helpful book, *The Shepherd Leader,* Tim Witmer points out that faithful shepherds have four primary responsibilities: *know the sheep, lead the sheep, protect the sheep,* and *feed the sheep.*[24]

Knowing the sheep

This means we know who is under our care and for whom we will give an account (Heb. 13:17). Peter says we are to shepherd the flock that is "among you" (1 Pet. 5:2). Previously, he said that Christians should not suffer as a "meddler" (4:15). This word *allotriepiskopos* comes from two root words: *allotrios* (belonging to another) and *episkopos* (overseer). The meaning is something like "one who watches over that which belongs to another." Or to say it another way, it's pastoring where you don't belong. If that were a problem in the first century, imagine what Peter would say about those who do this for hours on social media. As leaders of local churches, we should avoid being busybodies and focus on shepherding the church the Lord has allowed us to lead and serve. Know your church's macro weaknesses as well as the needs of individuals. Have a strategy and plan for keeping up with needs in the church and ways for people to receive pastoral care.

Leading the sheep

To lead God's sheep involves applying the New Testament's vision of the church to one's local context. It means having a clear and executable mission. It involves making wise decisions that build up the entire church. It involves equipping others for ministry and delegating certain responsibilities. It means giving counsel for others to follow. It means developing other leaders. And in all of this, it involves setting an example for others to follow (1 Pet. 5:3; Heb. 13:7).

Feeding the sheep

It is fundamental to feed God's sheep, for if sheep don't eat, they won't survive. I don't want to sound uncaring, but as someone told me early in ministry, it does no good to pet the sheep if you don't feed the sheep! Expounding Scripture weekly nourishes God's people (1 Pet. 1:23–2:3; John 21:15–19). God builds his church by his Word, so let us give ourselves to substantive, biblical, Christ-exalting, Spirit-empowered preaching! Feed the sheep as you administer the Lord's Supper, reflecting on the gospel deeply. Feed the sheep in your discipleship courses, small-group ministries, and in your mentoring of others.

Protecting the sheep

Protecting God's sheep is also a responsibility of the elders. "Fierce wolves" exist, and so we must be on our guard (Acts 20:28–30). We must give public instruction that involves warning people about the dangers of false teaching. Further, we protect the sheep by practicing healthy church discipline (see, for example, Matt. 18:15–20) as we guard the church's purity. Sometimes church discipline doesn't get to the ultimate step of exclusion (Matt. 18:17) because private warning achieves the purpose of restoring a wayward brother or sister (Matt. 18:15–16; Gal. 6:1).

As you look at this list of responsibilities, consider how the Chief Shepherd has done each for us. He knows us, feeds us, leads us, and protects us. Let us rely on him, as we serve as his undershepherds.

The heart of a godly shepherd

In a concise manner, Peter tells us how to shepherd "not under compulsion, but willingly, as God would have you; not for shameful gain, but eagerly; not domineering over those in your charge, but being examples to the flock" (1 Pet. 5:2b–3). These are some of the most prominent temptations for pastoral leaders today.

Not out of compulsion, but willingly

No one should have to force someone to be a pastor. This should be something to which a pastor aspires (1 Tim. 3:1). Moreover, we should do our work gladly, not coldly or grudgingly. Whether it's pastoral counseling, sermon preparation, or a staff meeting, let us never lose the wonder of grace, and so do our work happily unto the Lord.

This means that we must tend to our hearts so that we don't begrudge the regular duties of pastoral ministry. To be sure, there will be times in which we may not be in the best mood! "Willingness" means that we will do our job even in those times. In season or out of season, the faithful shepherd attends to his sacred responsibilities.

But if we feel a prolonged period of drudgery-based duty, instead of glad willingness, we need to revisit the gospel afresh. In light of God's mercy and grace toward us, we should stand in awe of the fact that we're in the ministry (cf. 2 Cor. 4:1). It's not that we *have* to attend another elder meeting, or prepare another sermon, or lead the prayer meeting—we *get* to do these things. So when we feel like the work is overly laborious, we should confess this to the Lord and ask for renewed joy. We should seek out other brothers and sisters for support and encouragement. And we should examine our lives to see if we are making sufficient space for rest and recreation.

Not for shameful gain, but eagerly

One famous baseball player once said that he would play for free simply because he loved the game so much. Many pastoral leaders do ministry with little to no compensation for the sheer love of Christ and the church. However, countless stories could be told about church scandals related to shameful gain. We must guard our hearts against greed (cf. Luke 12:15; 1 Tim. 3:3; 6:5; Tit. 1:7; 2 Pet. 2:14), and we should also not play favorites with the congregation based upon one's financial ability.

If you are an aspiring planter/pastor or a young ministry leader, please keep a close watch on your love for selfish gain as you grow older. The pattern I have observed is that one initially enters ministry out of sheer love for it, but over time, our hearts can be drawn away to selfish desires. Dan Dorani says, "It's one thing to *make* money, another to *serve* it."[25] We should guard against this drift, and we should also be aware of the relentless attacks of the enemy who wants to devour us (1 Pet. 5:8). The devil has a history of using shameful gain as one of his main allurements. Let us cultivate hearts of grace and generosity and selflessness so that we are not consumed in this way.

Not domineering, but rather setting a humble example

Toxic church environments exist today because of domineering, bullying pastors. Such behavior is totally out of line with Jesus' model of servant leadership

(Mark 10:42–45). It's not always greed or lust that destroys one's ministry; sometimes, it's power. These ungodly leaders are characterized by being manipulative, overbearing, micromanaging, and hyper-controlling. But this is not the way of Christ!

Leadership in the church is not lordship over people. It's about following Jesus and setting people an example to follow. If you are a younger planter / pastor, this cannot be overstated enough (cf. 1 Tim. 4:12). To paraphrase John Stott, "People will be less likely to despise your youth if they admire your example."[26]

In a striking parallel reference about ministry leadership, Paul says, "Not that we lord it over your faith, but we work with you for your joy, for you stand firm in your faith" (2 Cor. 1:24). So Paul's goal was the believer's joy (cf. Phil. 1:25). There are ten thousand things you could do for someone, but here is a crystal-clear verse about what we long to see in our kids, our small groups, our church, and in our mission—that people may delight in Jesus.

However, notice how Paul went about doing this. He didn't exercise lordship but rather worked with the Corinthians. It was cooperation, not domination. He believed in persuasion but not coercion. He had a responsibility to work, but he also understood the believers have a role to play in spiritual growth. Faithful leaders are not tyrants. We do the hard work of teaching, encouraging, guiding, counseling, and giving a godly example, but we don't micromanage people's lives. We must avoid being meddlesome, overbearing, hyper-controlling leaders—forgetting God has to do this work, and believers have to take their faith seriously.

Our reward

Church planting and pastoral ministry is hard work. Paul's metaphors for ministry involved things like a hard-working farmer, a dedicated soldier, and a disciplined athlete (2 Tim. 2:1–7). So how can we endure when people leave our church, when the soil is hard, when the church isn't growing, when we are criticized, when we are attacked, and when we encounter great discouragement? We have to keep our eyes on Jesus, the Chief Shepherd, who will reward his faithful servants.

During the pandemic, I kept telling our church that our hope is not in "returning to normal"; it is in the return of Christ and the new creation to come. That's what we are most looking forward to! And when our Lord appears, faithful saints will receive "the unfading crown of glory" (1 Pet. 5:4). The moment we lose sight of this eschatological vision, we can be overcome with the challenges of ministry. But investing in others is worth it when you keep this big picture in mind: Jesus giving you an unfading crown of glory (and not a leafy crown, as worn in the early athletic games). Never lose the wonder of this reality, dear church planter, pastor, or ministry leader. When you see Jesus on that day, you will not regret having shepherded the flock of God faithfully. May we stay low and dependent on him, as we seek him for grace until that day (1 Pet. 5:5).

You cannot always make people happy in your leadership. Some will misunderstand you, be critical of you, or oppose you. How do we continue on, then? We need to maintain a clean conscience before God (2 Cor. 1:12–14) and make it our aim to please the Lord (2 Cor. 5:9; 2 Tim. 2:4). Maintain a clean conscience by having godly motives for ministry and by pursuing a godly lifestyle. Please the Lord by keeping the Chief Shepherd ever before your eyes—the One who lived and died and rose for you; the One who is interceding for you right now; and the One who is coming again in glory.

Conclusion

Elders are entrusted with the task of shepherding God's flock as undershepherds of the Chief Shepherd, Jesus. This work involves knowing, leading, feeding, and protecting the sheep. Peter shows us what kind of motivation we must avoid and the kinds of motivations we should have in performing this noble task. While pastoral leadership is hard work, planters and pastors should keep their eyes on Jesus, who loves the church, strengthens undershepherds, and promises a reward to those who lead faithfully.

Reflection questions

1. What is mostly on your mind—a strategic missional plan for starting the church *or* how you

would pastor those God brings into the church you plant? Where do you feel weakest and how could you prepare well for both?

2. What benefits do you see in planting with another pastorally qualified person? What could be challenging about that? How would you seek to overcome those challenges and team together well?

3. How have you sought to equip others for ministry? Are there individuals you could point to where you can see the fruitfulness of your work in equipping them for ministry?

4. How would you hope to develop other leaders in the life of this new church (pastors, planters, and missionaries)?

7

Spiritual Maturity

It's very easy for individuals to rise to leadership in the church because of their gifting and charisma. But if a ministry leader's gifting surpasses his or her maturity, then that person is a walking disaster zone. Unfortunately, stories of moral failure abound because of this very issue: a failure to grow in godliness.

Ongoing growth in spiritual maturity (or personal godliness) is an absolute necessity for ministry leaders for at least three reasons: (1) godliness pleases God; (2) the qualifications for pastoral ministry revolve primarily around character and godliness, not gifting (with the exception of being able to teach); and (3) godliness makes up for a lot of our deficiencies in ministry.[27]

All Christians are called to live out Christ-like character, but pastors are to set the believers an example in this area, living a life above reproach. We must also be mindful of the enemy, who desires to devour church leaders in this very area. Daily, we must put sin to death and seek to grow in Christlikeness.

One of the classic passages we should regularly return to for self-examination and repentance is Colossians 3:1–17. Here, Paul exhorts the church to walk in their new identity and pursue spiritual maturity.

Our new identity

Paul begins with, "If then [or, Since then] you have been raised with Christ ..." (Col. 3:1). This "if then" statement harkens back to Paul's previous statement in Colossians 2:12–13 on how the believer has been raised to new life with Christ. We should never get over the wonder of being made alive, forgiven, and changed by God's power through the work of Christ. A number of glorious truths now apply to us.

We share in Christ's resurrection victory

As Paul reflects on the believer's new identity, he says we share in Christ's resurrection victory. We have been *raised with Christ* (Col. 3:1b). This little word "with" is the prefix "syn"—like synching up your phone with your iPad or computer. We have been synched up with Christ! What is true of him is true of us. We died with him, we have been raised with him, and in some mysterious way, we have already been seated with him (Eph. 2:4–7).

Recently, my favorite baseball team won the World Series. Several people came up to me and said, "Congratulations on the Nationals winning the Series!" I was like, "Thanks, but I didn't play ... I tried to coach, but no one seemed to listen when I yelled at them!" In a greater way, you really are *with* Christ. You really do share in his resurrection victory. You are not a fan of resurrection victory but a participant in it. This gives us great hope, great confidence about the future, and is the source of power for walking in godliness.

A new priority

Our new identity means we also have a new priority: *"seek the things that are above*, where Christ is, seated at the right hand of God. *Set your minds on things that are above*, not on things that are on earth" (Col. 3:1b–2, my emphasis). This means that we think on Christ's interests, his authority, his rule, and his reign. And as pastors, our role is to keep our focus and our people's focus there.

Christ being "seated at the right hand of God" recalls Psalm 110, an important psalm cited throughout the New Testament to speak of Christ's reign and his intercession. This sovereign rule of Christ should give us peace amid the challenges in life and ministry.

A new security

Additionally, our new identity means that we have a new security: "For you have died, and your life is hidden with Christ in God" (Col. 3:3). We have died to our old way of life, and that death has led to our liberty and a new security. We are secure and *safe in Christ*. It doesn't mean we won't have hardships. It means that Jesus will keep us in the midst of it all.

A new destiny

There's also a not-yet aspect of our Christian identity: "When Christ who is your life appears, then you also will appear with him in glory" (Col. 3:4). Being united to Christ means we also have a new destiny. Ministry requires that we keep this long view ever before us.

Look at this phrase: "Christ who is your life." As Christians, we died and have taken on a new life. Many people would prefer to put something in place of Christ: money, power, cars, achievements, or beauty. For the believer, *Christ* is our life (cf. Phil. 1:21)—everything centers on him.

But Christ is not just our life; he is also *our hope*. Notice the phrase "then you also," and that little word "with." When Paul thinks of Christ's glory, he thinks of Christ's people being with him! Have you ever received entrance into a special place because you were with someone important? You had no right to be there, but you got access because you were that person's plus one, as they say. So it is here—we will share in Christ's glory because we are with him. This had to encourage the Christians in Colossae, and it should encourage us as well. When the days are long in ministry, remember we will share in this glory.

When it comes to spiritual maturity, we must always come back to our new identity. Before we are ministry leaders, we are Christians! Our identity is not in what we do, in how big our church is, or in how many books we write. *Christ* is our life! We must remember who we are, what is ours, and all that will be ours in Christ. From this place of holy awareness and profound gratitude, we then seek to put sin to death and put on the virtues of Christ.

Put off all that is inconsistent with your new life in Christ

We often want to know what the dress code is. Casual. Smart casual. Business casual. Formal. Semi-formal. Festive. It can be very stressful, can't it? Sometimes we are told to just "look nice." "Wear something comfortable." A new word on the street for your attire or immense swag is "your drip." NBA rookie Tyler Hero said he had "the best drip" in the house at the NBA draft, referring to his outfit. Fashion (or lack of) has become a form of amusement at the NBA draft.

Whether or not you are fashionable or have the best drip, there's good news for all of us: the real clothes that matter are those described in Colossians 3:5–17. Every Christian can wear these clothes now because they are new creations in Christ.

However, Paul begins with a vice list of attitudes and actions that must not be part of our life (Col. 3:5–9).

Sensuality, greed, and sinful attitudes and speech

Paul first notes temptations relevant to all Christians and those that ministry leaders must watch out for: sensuality and greed (3:5–7) and sins related to sinful attitudes and speech (3:8–9).

He uses intense language when addressing what we must do with these temptations: "Put to death ..." (3:5). We aren't to try and simply get sin under control, but to kill it. One pastor told a story of a church member who showed up every week to the prayer meeting and prayed the same thing each week: "Oh Lord, the old spider of sin, the old spider of sin has been weaving its web; it's been weaving its web. Lord, break the web, break the web." Eventually, one night, when the older man prayed this again, the pastor shouted out, "No, Lord, kill the spider!"[28] We must seek to put our sin to death and lead others to do the same!

Paul goes on to say, "Put ... away" (3:8). Don't play around with sin—with your old life. Put it to death and put it away! Consider that way of life over! If you have played video games, you are aware of that message that comes up: "GAME OVER." We, too, need to move on and consider our former sinful ways to be over, and to lead others to do the same.

Specifically, Paul says we must put these sins to death: sexual immorality, impurity, passion (lust), evil desire, and covetousness (3:5). Pastors are explicitly urged not to be motivated by greed (cf. 1 Pet. 5:2; 1 Tim. 3:2; Tit. 1:7). And sadly, most of us know stories of ministry leaders who have fallen into sexual immorality and are no longer in ministry. Once again, we must put sin to death.

These sins are inconsistent with our new life. Christ has given us a new cleanness positionally, so let us live clean lives practically by confessing sin, seeking forgiveness from sin, and fighting sin.

How serious are these sins? Paul says, "On account of these the wrath of God is coming" (Col. 3:6). These sins provoke God's wrath (see Numbers 25 for one of many illustrations).

In verses 7–8, Paul tells us what we must remember: "In these you too once walked" (3:7), "But now" (3:8) we don't have to walk this way any longer! We're new. We're different. We have been raised to life! Therefore, you are not without hope if you are entangled in these sins. New creations can put these things to death! That doesn't mean it's easy, which is one of the reasons you need to be in biblical community, and one of the reasons team ministry is so valuable. I am greatly blessed by being able to confess my sin and pray with other guys on our church staff, who then spur me on to holiness. As church leaders, we must fight not only against sin but also against isolation. We must guard our hearts and allow others to get involved in our lives. It's much easier to talk about our church or ministry ideas than about our personal lives, but this is necessary for us to "watch our life and doctrine closely" (1 Tim. 4:16, NIV).

Relational sin

Paul's next list of sins generally falls under the relational sin category: "... anger, wrath, malice, slander, and obscene talk from your mouth. Do not lie to one another" (Col. 3:8b–9a). These verses speak to those who cannot control their temper or their tongue. Since Christ gives us a new calmness, we can put aside anger—another great temptation for those in ministry. When people are critical of you, you need to apply the gospel to your heart so that you don't retaliate in anger, arrogance, and sinful speech.

The good news is that since Christ has brought us into the light, we can put aside sinful speech. Sadly, gossip and slander are perhaps the most acceptable sins in the church and can be observed in too many church leaders' lives. This should not be! Great churches are led by honest and honorable servants.

Why should we adopt this pursuit of godliness? It is because "you have put off the old self with its practices and have put on the new self" (3:9b–10a). Since we are new and are "being renewed" (3:10), live in a way consistent with this reality. The phrase "image of its creator" (3:10b) recalls Colossians 1:15, where Paul says that Christ is "the image of the invisible God." Christians are being renewed in the image of Christ. That's what it means to live a godly life—to look like Jesus.

A practical implication for this new life is the *unity* of believers (3:11). Paul told the Colossian church that in Christ, racial, ethnic, and social barriers are broken down (cf. Gal. 3:28). As pastors who desire for harmony to exist amid our diversity, the issue of godliness must be exemplified and taught to our people.

Verse 11 ends with a Christological climax: "Christ is all, and in all" (Col. 3:11). This is the declaration of one who is growing in godliness. Christ is all to us, and Christ unites us together. We get to tell our congregation of this unity each time we take the Lord's Supper, a powerful means of renewing our minds in the gospel.

Put on all that is consistent with your new life in Christ

In Colossians 3:12–17, we should see the *community emphasis* of this text. Every believer has a responsibility to obey these verses, but the thrust of the text is *corporate*. The traits of verses 12–14 are to replace the sins that divide the body, which were noted in verses 8–9. Thus "peace" (3:15) is to characterize the body, with an obvious "one another" emphasis in verse 16. We should also see the *replacement focus* of this text. We are to throw off anger and sinful speech, replacing these sins with compassion, kindness, forgiveness, and so on. The Christian and the Christian community are to be known not only by what we reject but by what we practice. As church leaders, we have the high calling to lead our church in this process of spiritual maturity.

To summarize these verses, the inspired apostle tells us that the character of Christ should adorn us (3:12–14); the peace of Christ should rule us (3:15); the Word of Christ should transform us (3:16); and the name of Christ should motivate us (3:17). It's helpful to turn these into prayers for our church.

May the character of Christ adorn us

May Christ's character clothe us as we display compassion, kindness, humility, meekness, and patience. Christ is known for these virtues, and Christ's followers must pursue them. Paul adds that we are to be "bearing with one another" and "forgiving each other" (3:13). Forgiveness is to be extended and experienced because "the Lord has forgiven you" (3:13). As a pastor, I need to keep coming back to the gospel because I can be tempted to harbor unforgiveness. But this does not please God; it does not strengthen the church. Paul tells the Corinthians that unforgiveness is one way Satan seeks to divide and destroy the church (2 Cor. 2:11). We must not let him have the upper hand but must forgive as we have been forgiven (Eph. 4:32).

This idea of "bearing with one another" is important because there are some problematic people in Christ's church! A mark of spiritual maturity is the ability not only to forgive sin but also to overlook basic frustrations with others. Growing in maturity involves growing in mercy and compassion and love. Paul prioritizes love in the next verse: "Above all these put on love, which binds everything together in perfect harmony" (Col. 3:14; cf. 1 Cor. 16:14). As ministry leaders, we must follow Christ in the way of love (John 13:1–20) and lead our people to walk in love also (cf. Gal. 5:22; Rom. 12:9; 1 Cor. 13).

May the peace of Christ rule us

Another sign of maturity is the ability to deal with conflict properly. When Christ's peace rules in our hearts, it will work itself out into cultivating peaceful relationships. His peace should reign in our relationships with others (cf. Jam. 3:13–18). Why were we "called in one body" (Col.

3:15)? It was with this goal: peace. We didn't establish or create peaceful unity—Christ did that—but we are to maintain it. So then, as a ministry leader, let the peace of Christ be your goal in relationships, doing your best to be a peacemaker!

There is one more thing to note: Paul says, "And be thankful" (3:15). Here, thankfulness is associated with "peace." I take this to mean we are to be thankful for the peace Christ brings (for it is a gift of grace) and to let this gift be an incentive for maintaining peace.

May the Word of Christ dwell richly in us

The peace of Christ rules in our hearts when the Word of Christ dwells richly in us (3:16). "The word of Christ"— that is, *the message of Christ* (that's what the Word is about!)—needs to be at home in us. Don't let the Word of Christ be an occasional visitor, but let it settle down and transform you. Don't just study the Word for sermons and lessons, but let it dwell richly in you as you meditate on it daily. We will not grow in maturity apart from by the living Word.

Here again, the focus goes corporate. We are to let the Word dwell in us richly as we do something: *teach and admonish one another*. This doesn't mean there are no formal roles of teaching and pastoring, but this text is one of those passages that emphasizes how every believer should be instructing and encouraging one another with the Word of Christ (cf. Rom. 15:14). Paul says that one of the ways we instruct and encourage is through *psalms, hymns, and spiritual songs* (Col. 3:16). People often try to differentiate between three types of songs here, but I think a rigid distinction is unnecessary. The important aspect is that we sing, that our singing should have rich variety, and that this singing is about the message of Christ. Further, there is a sense of joyfulness that should be part of the Christian church: "with thankfulness in your hearts to God" (3:16). As Christ's Word is expounded and sung, true wisdom transforms us.

May the name of Christ motivate us

Paul finishes this powerful passage by reminding the saints, "And whatever you do, in word or deed, do everything in the name of the Lord Jesus, giving thanks to God the Father through him" (3:17). This means to be conscious of his calling of you. Remember who you are! His name represents his character. You bear Christ's name. It means to be aware of his sovereign presence and to depend on him at all times, in life and ministry. It means always to be mindful of his instructions.

This is our great motivation for planting and pastoring: Christ's name. We want to honor Christ by the power of Christ, displaying the character of Christ.

Conclusion

Christian maturity involves us embracing and rejoicing in our new identity in Christ. Out of this heart, we are to be putting off all that is inconsistent with our new life in Christ while putting on all that is consistent with our new life. Church planters and ministry leaders are to model growth in maturity and lead others to grow in godliness. Not every leader has the same gifting, but all have this calling to grow in Christlikeness and spur God's people on to do the same.

Reflection questions

1. What areas of your life have seen God grow you in maturity? Where are you still weak?

2. How have you observed a life of godliness make up for deficiencies in your ministry giftedness?

3. How have you experienced the grace of God in seeking to put to death those things in you that are inconsistent with your new life in Christ (related to sensuality, greed, sinful attitudes, speech, and relationships)?

4. How would you apply the gospel toward cultivating unity in diversity across ethnic, linguistic, social, and economic lines when starting a church?

8

Missional Lifestyle

Another way planters and pastors lead by example is by living a missional lifestyle. There are various ways this might be done, but I want to highlight two: (1) ministering with gospel intentionality within one's already existing networks, and (2) practicing hospitality.

I want to think through these two ways of Christian witness because everyone can do this kind of evangelism. None of our members may preach at a massive crusade, nor does every Christian feel comfortable doing cold-call evangelism, but every Christian can live with gospel intentionality and practice kingdom-minded hospitality.

Living with gospel intentionality in our networks

Everyone has a web of relationships, but we often fail to think about intentionally reaching the people right in front of us. Evangelism is often seen as adding "something additional" to your life, but a missional lifestyle involves identifying the people in your web of relationships and seeking to engage them in a variety of ways.

The more and more secular certain contexts become, the more and more we have to think about reaching people outside the church walls. Most unbelievers have no interest in attending our Sunday church services at Imago Dei. In our Western, post-Christian world, we need more than a cool venue, specialty roasted coffee, good music, or dynamic preaching to attract non-believers. If any unbelievers are present in our worship gatherings, chances are someone befriended and invited them outside the church walls, like in the shopping centers, workplaces, neighborhoods, or recreational spaces, or even in our families. In other words, we evangelize those in our networks. Let me share some reasons to emphasize this method of mission.

Network evangelism recognizes the sovereignty of God

When you identify the people in your sphere of influence, you should recognize that God has you where you are for his sovereign purposes. It's no accident who you work with, play with, or shop with. God has us living in this time and place in history, surrounded by image bearers that he has sovereignly put in our path (cf. Acts 17:26–27).

Network evangelism has historic precedent

In his book *Cities of God*, sociologist Rodney Stark describes how Christianity became an urban movement and conquered Rome:

[S]ocial networks are the basic mechanism through which conversion takes place ... Most conversions are not produced by professional missionaries conveying a new message, but by rank-and-file members who share their faith with their friends and relatives ... The principle that conversions spread through social networks is quite consistent with the fact that the earliest followers of Jesus shared many family ties and long-standing associations ... Although the very first Christian converts in the West may have been by full-time missionaries, the conversion process soon became self-sustaining as new converts accepted the obligation to spread their faith and did so by missionizing their immediate circle of intimates.[29]

"Ordinary members" of the church lived with gospel intentionality among their social networks then, and we need to promote this practice today.

Network evangelism promotes steadfastness and patience in evangelism

Often, it takes a long time for an unbeliever to embrace Jesus as Lord. Some methods of evangelism can come across as being numbers-driven rather than people-driven. If you're reaching people in your networks, then you have to keep loving them and listening to them.

So the question that every Christian should ask is, "Who are the people in my networks?" It has been helpful for our church to think within these five categories:

1. Familial network—people in your family

2. Geographical network—people in
   your neighborhood

3. Vocational network—people at the workplace

4. Recreational network—people with whom you
   play or hang out with

5. Commercial network—people you see at shops

We have encouraged our people to try to identify at least *five people* in each of these networks—or if they are low in one area, to increase the number of people in the other networks. And we have encouraged them to do *one of five tasks*: (1) pray for them (you may be surprised at what will happen if you simply start this!); (2) invite them (into your home, to a restaurant, or to a church service); (3) serve them (look for ways to bless them); (4) give resources to them (such as books or podcasts); and (5) share the gospel with them (look for opportunities to explain the good news). While we eventually need to get to number five with unbelievers, these five practices give every Christian a pathway to living on mission. At the very least, every Christian can pray for unbelievers they know.

Get hopeful!
Regarding the task of sharing the gospel, I find Peter's words very timely for living out a missional lifestyle among our networks:

> *Now who is there to harm you if you are zealous for what*
> *is good? But even if you should suffer for righteousness'*
> *sake, you will be blessed. Have no fear of them, nor be*
> *troubled, but in your hearts honor Christ the Lord as holy,*
> *always being prepared to make a defense to anyone who*
> *asks you for a reason for the hope that is in you; yet do it*
> *with gentleness and respect, having a good conscience, so*
> *that, when you are slandered, those who revile your good*
> *behavior in Christ may be put to shame. For it is better to*
> *suffer for doing good, if that should be God's will, than*
> *for doing evil. (1 Pet. 3:13–17)*

Peter doesn't give us a kind of formula to follow. Rather, he focuses on the heart and the life of faithful witnesses, and on the everyday nature of a faithful witness.[30]

He points out that we should always be ready to share the reason for our *hope*. Christian hope (which involves a steady confidence and delight in God's blessings for us now and in the future) is a vital virtue to cultivate, not only for our own faithfulness but also for our own witness.

The word "defense" (3:15) is the Greek word *apologia*, from which we get "apologetics." At one level, this does demand some level of study ("reason" calls for logical thought, and to be "prepared" implies study). But Peter's not describing formal, academic apologetics or debating in a public setting. He has an ordinary conversation in mind. For us, that may be at work, in the gym, at the store, or while walking a neighborhood. Peter has in mind Christians being ready to explain why Christ is more precious than anything, and explaining why we have hope beyond the grave. Every Christian can do this because all Christians have this hope! There is a lot of negativity and despair in the world, and unbelievers can often spot this unique hope that shines forth from us. In other words, Peter calls us to live out an apologetic of hope in this world among the people God puts in our path.

This hope, then, flows from our adoration of Jesus. This is very important when thinking about mission. To be a good and faithful witness, you need to adore Christ. You need to be filled with hope every day. And one of the ways this hope will be communicated is when *we suffer*. We can enter into conversation with unbelievers, telling them about our hope. Or, we can communicate this hope when *they are suffering*. Often evangelism looks more like counseling than street preaching. With "gentleness and respect" (3:15), we can share our hope with those with whom we interact.

Practicing hospitality

Practicing hospitality is a wonderful way to do both mercy ministry and to share the hope within us. Recall that inviting people is one of my five ways to reach those in your networks. This practice also remains a culturally appropriate way to bear witness (in most contexts). What's more, it's a reflection of our God, who has also commanded us (extroverts and introverts alike!) to be hospitable (Rom. 12:13; 1 Pet. 4:9; cf. Lev. 19:33–34). For those aspiring to pastoral leadership, it's also a qualification for an overseer (1 Tim. 3:2; Tit. 1:8).[31]

God the Host

Like most things in the Christian life, we often struggle with motivation. That's why we should regularly think about the hospitality of God. It will increase both our love for others and our willingness to open up our homes and our lives to people.

In the garden, God provided a home and made provision for Adam and Eve. In Exodus, God miraculously provided food and water as Israel wandered in the wilderness; he told them to remember his deliverance through a Passover meal. Further, he took them to the "land flowing with milk and honey" (Ex. 3:8). God welcomes, hosts, cares for, provides for, and blesses.

Fast forward to the New Testament and we see Jesus constantly eating with people! He gets labeled as a "glutton and a drunkard, a friend of tax collectors and sinners" (Luke 7:34). He hangs out with the hated, with all sorts of scoundrels, like Levi and Zacchaeus. Lots of ministry was done around the table.

It's also striking to see the early church's practice of hospitality. They gathered in homes for worship, and did a lot of ministry in homes (see, for example, Acts 2:46; 10:24; 16:13–15, 30–34; 20:20; Rom. 16:1–15; 1 Cor. 16:19).

In the book of Revelation, we see a glorious vision of God's people at the great wedding banquet (Rev. 19:7) and with God dwelling with his people (Rev. 22). The book ends with an invitation for the "thirsty to come" to God and be satisfied forever (22:17). What a gracious, hospitable God!

Be a good host

Practically speaking, every Christian, especially those who are called to lead by example, should work at the art of Christian hospitality. Let me share some things I have learned from others and areas I want to grow in personally.

First, expand your guest list. Recall Jesus' words:

> *He said also to the man who had invited him, "When you give a dinner or a banquet, do not invite your friends or your brothers or your relatives or rich neighbors, lest they also invite you in return and you be repaid. But when you give a feast, invite the poor, the crippled, the lame, the blind, and you will be blessed, because they cannot repay you. For you will be repaid at the resurrection of the just." (Luke 14:12–14)*

Jesus says that when you have a big event, invite those who can't repay you. Invite the marginalized. If you do this, you will be repaid "at the resurrection of the just"! Jesus fills up ordinary events, like having people over to your home, with eternal significance.

Second, serve others; don't try to impress them. Hospitality is not about showing off but about welcoming, loving, and caring for others. As I have talked with people about using their homes to do ministry, I have found that many people simply overthink this. You can do hospitality with paper plates and a simple meal.

Third, while you need some space to rest and retreat in your home, avoid thinking that your house is your refuge. We only have one refuge, and that's our great God (Ps. 46:1)! We need to be good stewards of everything the Lord has given us, and one of those things is a home. If you have small living quarters, you can consider other ways to welcome and host, such as by showing people around town or going out for coffee.

Fourth, pay attention to what people like or need. Take notice of what they eat, drink, and get excited about. You can make a great connection by surprising people with these favorite items, and it can lead to some great conversations. Pay attention to any need they may have and offer to help. For example, lend a hand with a home project, help them to fix their car or some other machine, or offer to dog sit. This, too, can really build relationships. We recently got to know our neighbors simply by collecting their mail and taking out their trash when they went out of town. They came back and showed up with a thank you gift for us.

Fifth, consider your own context and skills and make a plan. My wife currently hosts a monthly book club at our house for our neighbors. This is not a "Christian book club," but a group of ladies in our neighborhood reading popular books. They eat and talk about the monthly selection. Perhaps you love cooking and want to host regular dinner parties. You could have a board game night where you invite neighbors and coworkers over to play games. Maybe you can coach a local sport and so get to know kids and families. Alternatively, you could host a kickball game in the park on Saturdays, or even just set up a simple basketball goal and some refreshments. It's amazing how sports attract kids. The list goes on. Densely urban areas will differ from suburban and rural areas. Dangerous areas will differ from safer ones. To think like a missionary means to think about doing ministry well in your particular context.

Sixth, consider practicing hospitality with others. Sometimes it works well if one person is the host and someone else leads the conversation. Introverts and extroverts can unite in faithful hospitality!

Finally, learn to greet people warmly, engage them sincerely, and say goodbye thoughtfully. The greetings and farewells in the New Testament are filled with warmth and meaning (see, for example, Acts 20:36; 21:5–6; Rom. 16:16). When someone comes into your home, greet them affectionately. Take their coat. Offer them a drink. Give them a place to sit. Don't stay on the couch and yell for them to come inside! As you have conversation, ask questions about the guest's life. Don't turn everything back on yourself. Put your phone away. Whenever the visit is over, walk the guests to the door, and even to their car (or train or bus stop), when possible. All of these gestures are meant to convey value and love, and people remember them.

This is not an exhaustive list, but hopefully a helpful one. We should always keep learning ways to be more faithful in this ancient Christian practice.

Conclusion

Living a missional lifestyle involves living with gospel intentionality. God has sovereignly put people in our path, in our various networks. We have the privilege of praying for them, serving them, inviting them into our homes and churches, giving gospel resources to them, and sharing the hope of the gospel with them. One of the practical ways we can have a meaningful ministry with unbelievers is by practicing hospitality, a practice fueled by God's gracious hospitality. This is a practice we should always be learning more about so we can become more faithful witnesses in our context.

Reflection questions

1. How are you cultivating meaningful relationships with those around you who do not yet belong to Christ?

2. How are you practicing evangelism? How often do you personally share the gospel with unbelievers? Can you share a recent example of this?

3. Have you been able to appropriately adapt to another cultural context in order to befriend

someone and minister the hope of the gospel to them? Can you share a time when you made an effort to take the gospel across cultural barriers?

4. How has practicing hospitality been a means for the spread of the gospel with those God has placed around you?

9

Disciple-Making

Our church has a lot of young families, and we have something like a child born every twelve days! (We're living up to our name, "Imago Dei"!) We also have had the privilege of sending a number of folks out as church planters and missionaries, both domestically and globally. So I have found myself on multiple occasions having serious missional conversations with someone while at the same time trying to interact with one of our wonderful kids, who is vying for my attention. One time, I was talking to a young, single woman preparing to relocate to the Middle East to reach Muslim women. Suddenly, I had this little guy pulling my arm, saying, "I can do the moonwalk! I can do the moonwalk!" After telling him, "Let me see!" (it was really good!), this question popped into my mind: "How can we get this little moonwalker to the mission field?" It will take a lot of discipleship.

Every Christian is called to make Jesus' last command our first priority: to make disciples among the nations (Matt. 28:18–20). This involves both reaching and teaching people, both locally and globally. Disciple-making, simply defined, means "helping others follow Jesus."[32] Church planters and pastors lead the way in this and must equip others to do the same.

Jesus' Great Commission

The final chapter of Matthew's Gospel begins with the greatest news and ends with the greatest mission. Matthew links many of the first scenes of the Gospel with this last scene, connecting Christmas with Easter. At Jesus' birth, we read that he is called "Immanuel ... God with us" (1:23). At the end of Matthew, Jesus gives his disciples this promise, "I am with you always" (28:20). At his birth, Jesus is called the king of the Jews (2:2). At the end of the book, we read, "All authority in heaven and on earth has been given to me" (28:18). At Jesus' birth, wise men come from Gentile lands to worship him (2:1–12). In the final chapter, the disciples worship him, and Jesus sends them to the Gentiles (28:17). It's a wonderful conclusion.

Even though the Great Commission is an often-quoted text, we really can never hear it enough. One pastor shared an anecdote about it that has stuck with me. A widely acclaimed theology professor in Scotland had some of the stereotypical professor habits (strange mannerisms, a bit nerdy, and, in this case, a monocle in one eye). He was respected by many and even had many military distinctions. The faculty where he taught had regular chapter services, at which this professor would preach. Each time, he would preach from exactly the same text: Matthew 28:18–20. This certainly wasn't because he didn't know anything else. Rather, his focus illustrated the vital importance of Jesus' command to his followers.[33] It should remain ever before us.

Of course, this text has had a tremendous impact on many others throughout history, including William Carey, the "father of the modern missions movement." Carey's farewell address to his congregation before leaving for India was Matthew 28:16–20. He got the Great Commission, or perhaps we should say, "The Great Commission got him!" The question is, has it gotten us?

The central command: make disciples

The all-authoritative King, who is with us always, has given his people the command to make disciples. We cannot negotiate with the King but must submit to this charge. And we submit to it with *confidence* because he is with us, and ruling over all things. We also submit to him with *joy*, for who he is and what he has done for us and all that he has for us.

Technically, the one imperative of verse 19 is: "make disciples." Jesus doesn't say go "make decisions" (as important as decisions are), but "make disciples." Discipleship begins with a decision to follow Jesus, but the goal is total allegiance to him. The goal is not to make some more nominal Christians!

Tied to this imperative are three participles in the original Greek: "going, baptizing, and teaching" (28:19–20). They function like imperatives. The mandate is clear: make disciples by going, baptizing, and teaching.

Make disciples by going

The church is charged to engage the world. Church planters embody this spirit as they go into rural, suburban, or urban areas to make disciples and see a healthy, multiplying church established.

It has been said that the church is not a cruise ship but a troop carrier. Nothing is more "all about me" than a cruise ship! But the disciple of Jesus is sent on mission with the good news, seeking to reach unbelievers and grow them up into maturity.

When Jesus mentions going among "all nations" (28:19), he means all ethnic and language groupings of people. He has in mind "every tribe and language and people and nation" (Rev. 5:9). Thousands still need to hear the good news of Christ and be equipped to follow him.

Make disciples by baptizing

This has both a reaching and teaching component, as well. As evangelistic church planters, we want to see unbelievers confess, "Jesus is Lord!" We want to instruct them in such a way that they're ready to make a bold declaration to the world, through baptism, that they are followers of Jesus. This is a work of grace. As such, we baptize them in the name of our gracious, Triune God.

It is such a joy to see those we've been engaging with the gospel declare their allegiance to Jesus and begin growing in him. We should never lose the wonder of this miracle and constantly keep this mission before our people. Church planting is not about shuffling some disgruntled church members from one church to a new church! We must keep our eyes, and our people's eyes, on the harvest field in our context.

Make disciples by teaching

New believers need to be further taught, and that takes place primarily through the local church (Acts 2:1–47). The church is a family of learners and teachers. We cannot make disciples apart from teaching. Obviously, as a pastor, you need to be "able to teach" (1 Tim. 3:2), but we must also equip all God's people in teaching others how to follow Christ.

In our disciple-making, the point is not simply to transfer information to others. Rather, we want them to "observe" (obeying, keeping, and doing) all that Jesus has commanded (Matt. 28:20). In the words of James, we must show them how to be "doers of the word" (Jam. 1:22). The devil knows the Bible, but our goal is to teach people transformation. We are to teach "all" that Jesus has commanded, with this end in mind: that they may obey their Christ faithfully.

The work of disciple-making

The most popular text on disciple-making is the text we've just considered, which involves reaching unbelievers and nurturing them in the faith. Still, we have many other passages that highlight some of the other practical aspects of disciple-making.

Children

For starters, parents are called to disciple their children
(Eph. 6:1–4; cf. Deut. 6:4–9). Pastors must equip God's
people to do this well (Eph. 4:11ff). Pastors must also
not neglect the important role of discipling their own
children. At the dinner table, in car rides back home from
church services, on vacation, before bedtime, and in many
more places, parents have the holy privilege of explaining
and applying the gospel to their children. Further, church
members may also have wonderful opportunities to
train and mentor children through various ministries
in the church or through one-on-one mentoring. I have
witnessed many single people in our church significantly
impact some of our children.

Men and women, young and old

In the book of Titus, we read of the wonderful vision of
disciple-making in the church among men and women,
young and old (Tit. 2:1–10). Churches flourish when
every person is built up in their most holy faith. The
church is an intergenerational family (1 Tim. 5:1–2)
that has the privilege of teaching sound doctrine and
practical application for every life. This happens as men
and women of every age pursue God's design for their
lives (Tit. 2:1-10). We have seen this kind of discipleship
take place at our church in various ways, such as through
women's book clubs, men's prayer breakfasts, workdays,
special events, youth camps, and more.

Leaders

In Paul's second letter to Timothy, we find one of my favorite verses for equipping leaders: "and what you have heard from me in the presence of many witnesses entrust to faithful men, who will be able to teach others also" (2 Tim. 2:2). The need exists worldwide for this high-level disciple-making and equipping, as we seek to saturate the nations with faithful ministers who can teach God's Word. When we planted our church, we said that we would give time each week to 2 Timothy 2:2 ministry, even if we only had one or two people we were developing for church leadership and church planting. It's a vital ministry.

Biblical exposition

One of the primary ways church planters and pastors will disciple their congregations is through biblical exposition (cf. 2 Tim. 4:2). Some people wrongly assume you can't plant a church if you teach the Bible in-depth, but I would challenge that assumption! You do work hard to be clear, engaging, and accessible, but you don't need to water down your teaching. The temptation exists to attract a crowd on gimmicks or sensationalized antics, but our calling is not to draw a crowd but to build a church—to build a community of disciples. We cannot do that apart from substantive preaching and teaching (Acts 2:42; 11:25–26; 18:11; 19:10; 20:20, 27; 1 Pet. 4:11).

Pastoral care and counseling

Additionally, the work of pastoral care and counseling is an important aspect of discipleship. This work is unique as it deals with particular problems such as grief, abuse, conflict, anxiety, depression, addiction, and more. However, the goal is still to see people flourish and grow up into Christlikeness as we apply the gospel to their situation with truth and love (Eph. 4).

Discipling one another

Finally, church members are called to disciple one another. Paul told the Colossian church, "Let the word of Christ dwell in you richly, teaching and admonishing one another in all wisdom" (Col. 3:16a). And to the Romans he said, "I myself am satisfied about you, my brothers, that you yourselves are full of goodness, filled with all knowledge and able to instruct one another" (Rom. 15:14). Notice that Paul is happy ("satisfied") about the church because they are full of *goodness* (character), they are *knowledgeable* (they have been taught), and they can *instruct* one another. This may be done in one-on-one member care, a small Bible study, or some other context. However, our aim as church leaders is to teach in such a way that believers are able to disciple others also.

The idea that every Christian should be a disciple-maker means we need to raise the bar for believers. We need to tell them that they shouldn't just listen to sermons (which is good), nor simply be receivers of content (which is also good), but be *reproducers* of all that they're learning.

I was once on a panel discussion with Bill Hull, who has written and spoken on discipleship for many years. He told one of his classes on their first day, "I'm not going to test you at the end of the semester. I want you to go reteach someone else. Then I'm going to test them and give you whatever grade they receive!" That got their attention, and it illustrated the point he was trying to make. Christians are always learning and teaching, receiving and reproducing, absorbing and sharing—so we may make more and more healthy disciples who obey all that Jesus commanded.

Use all your golf clubs

Several years ago, I heard a golfing illustration about discipleship and the three ways we teach. As a church planter and pastor, you have the opportunity to use all your clubs—the woods, the irons, and the putter.

You could liken the woods, especially a driver, to preaching in corporate worship. The driver covers a lot of ground. It's big. It's visible. It's very good. You need a good driver. You could liken your irons to the kind of teaching that requires more dialogue than monologue. This is like a class or a small group. As a pastor, I have opportunities to teach in these settings as well—to our interns, membership class, and other classes. But there's one club that many pastors don't spend enough time on, and that's one-on-one discipleship or mentoring. You might liken it to the putter. A lot of pastors focus exclusively on their driver, but need to remember what good golfers say: "You drive for show and put for dough."

Please understand that I'm not minimizing preaching; I love it, believe in it, and teach it. We need a good driver. All I'm saying, as a disciple-making pastor, is there are more ways to teach than from the pulpit. Let's use all of our clubs! And let's not underestimate the work of discipleship others are doing in classes or one-on-one mentoring. Instead, let's encourage people in this good work.

Christ is with us

The call to disciple people is a lifelong task, and it will be challenging, especially in certain contexts. But the good news is that Jesus promises to be with us every step of the way. The King loves us.

The Great Commission can be seen in four great "alls." It's great not only because it includes the greatest *authority* ("all authority in heaven and on earth" has been given to Jesus), the greatest *mission field* ("all nations"), and the greatest *curriculum* ("all that" Jesus has "commanded"), but also because it comes with the greatest *assurance*: "I am with you always, to the end of the age," or "for all our days." It is worth giving our lives to this mission.

You probably feel unfit for this assignment, but just pause for a minute and consider who preserved the Great Commission for us: Matthew, the tax collector. He was a hated, despised, and crooked man. He was like a mafia member. But Jesus transformed him. Jesus told him, "Follow me," and he did!

Jesus makes sinners his disciples, who go and make more disciples. Every believer can mature as Matthew did. He matured so well he could pass on Jesus' words through this Gospel. I'm not saying you'll write the Bible—please don't! But you can communicate his Word to others. Jesus made Matthew a disciple-maker, and he continues to do this transformative work. The words and presence and power of Jesus changed Matthew, and Christ is bringing to completion the work that he started in us, until our work is done. He's with us. Now let's get on with it.

Conclusion

As disciple-making planters, pastors, and ministry leaders, we aim to help people follow Jesus. This involves the work of reaching unbelievers and helping them mature in the faith, that they, too, may be disciple-makers. This work involves going, baptizing, and teaching among all nations, with the local church being the primary place of seeing believers mature in the faith. This work can be done in a variety of ways, and it's work we do with confidence and joy because Jesus is with us, and has authority over all things.

Reflection questions

1. With the knowledge that Jesus' last command is to be our first priority (to make disciples of

all nations), how would you prioritize this in church planting?

2. Why is maturity and multiplication important in disciple-making? How would you foster both maturity and multiplication in the life of a new church?

3. Consider your own efforts to make disciples over the last two years. How have you sought to help present others mature in Christ (Col. 1:28)? Who can you point to as an example of your intentionality in disciple-making?

4. Consider the golf club analogy to discipling from the pulpit (driver), in the small group (irons), and one-on-one (putter). How would you seek to establish weekly and monthly rhythms in church planting where you can use all of your clubs in helping others to follow Jesus?

10

The Ability to Teach

A few years ago, I had the privilege of being with some Acts 29 leaders in Berlin for some meetings. On our day off, some of us took the train to the historic town of Wittenberg, Germany. From this little town, Martin Luther set the world on fire with his writings, publishing, teaching, and preaching.

There are many wonderful sights to behold in Wittenberg. However, perhaps my favorite spot is not where Luther lived, nor where he nailed the famous ninety-five theses, but where he frequently preached: St Mary's Church. I had visited Wittenberg a year before, so I could hardly wait until everyone else got to see where the reformer proclaimed and explained the gospel for many years. I also wanted them to see the paintings inside the church which artistically portray its various ministries.

The paintings inside are by Lucas Cranach, the famous artist during the Reformation.[34] My favorite is one depicting Luther preaching, which illustrates how we should view the Scriptures and how we should view biblical exposition. The picture shows Luther with one finger on the text and then with one finger pointing to Christ crucified. And the congregation's eyes are all fixed on Christ (not the preacher). As church planters and pastoral leaders, we get to carry on this great tradition.

While the pastoral qualifications for pastors in 1 Timothy 3:1–7 mainly focus on character, one speaks to a particular ability: the ability to teach (1 Tim. 3:2; cf. 2 Tim. 2:24; Tit. 1:9). This should come as no surprise to us because at the heart of our faith is the life-changing message of the gospel that must be heralded and taught, announced and explained.

Of course, every Christian is called to make disciples by "teaching" (Matt. 28:18–20), but pastoral leaders and planters must have particular skills in teaching. Paul's words to Titus give us more specifics as to what this means: "He must hold firm to the trustworthy word as taught, so that he may be able to give instruction in sound doctrine and also to rebuke those who contradict it" (Tit. 1:9). Notice three ideas here. First, pastors must have a thorough *knowledge* of sound doctrine. They need to be equipped theologically and be committed to their orthodox biblical convictions. Second, they must have the ability to *instruct* the church in sound doctrine, exhorting them to respond appropriately to it. Finally, they must have the ability to *rebuke* those who teach contrary to sound doctrine—in order to protect the church, and hopefully even to see the false teachers come to the knowledge of the truth.

For the church planter, the importance of proclaiming the gospel and explaining biblical doctrine cannot be overstated. To be sure, many other ministries deserve our attention, but we must never overlook the ministry of the Word (Acts 6:4). I recall a church-planting conference held several years ago that offered sessions on dozens of subjects, but didn't have a single session on preaching and teaching! A friend of mine had been asked to speak on a particular topic but asked if he could talk about the process of biblical exposition instead. This illustrates what can happen in church planting: that which is central to the health and vitality of the church can be pushed to the periphery. We must see to it that this never happens.

In 1 Timothy 4:11–16, Paul gives some important exhortations that help provide a comprehensive vision of the teaching ministry. After critiquing the false teacher's message (4:1–5), and after calling Timothy to train for godliness (4:6–10), Paul continues his challenge, saying, "Command and teach these things" (4:11). Here, he is referring to Timothy's task of passing on apostolic doctrine. Paul then highlights various aspects of a faithful teacher's task and his lifestyle. In doing so, he underscores the fact that faithful ministers lead with the Word and by example.

Exemplify your teaching personally

Paul urges Timothy to have his life shaped by the gospel, saying, "Let no one despise you for your youth, but set the believers an example in speech, in conduct, in love, in faith, in purity" (4:12). As many church planters are young, this verse is especially important. People were apparently critical of Timothy's youthfulness—he was probably in his thirties.[35]

It's not hard to imagine the kinds of challenges Timothy would have faced. People could have been jealous of his being promoted to leadership at a young age. They could have doubted his competency. They could have disrespected him. And it's not hard to imagine how Timothy would have wanted to respond if operating in the flesh: argumentatively, harshly, impatiently. (All these ways would have been the opposite of what Paul tells him to do in 2 Timothy 2:24–25.)

So how do you respond to criticism as a young minister? Not by hitting the social media sites and blasting away. Not by aggressive behavior. Not by fight or flight. It's by doing something altogether different: by setting the believers an example with your life. People will be less likely to despise your youth if they admire your example (cf. 1 Pet. 5:3).[36] The way you overcome the challenge of being criticized for your age is by Christlikeness, which includes speech and behavior graces (1 Tim. 4:12). So guard your tongue ("speech"). Watch your habits ("conduct"). Care for all the sheep ("love"). Show the church what trusting God looks like ("faith"). And pursue holiness ("purity"). Embody your doctrine. Apply your teaching to your own life.

Expound the Scriptures publicly

This is an important verse on many levels: "Until I come, devote yourself to the public reading of Scripture, to exhortation, to teaching" (4:13). You will show what you believe about the Bible by how you use the Bible, not merely what you say about it. If you want people to be convinced of the Scripture's authority, sufficiency, and Christocentricity, then expound the Bible faithfully and point them to Jesus consistently.

Interestingly, Paul follows up his word about Timothy's age with the exhortation to read, preach, and teach Scripture. Our authority as ministers doesn't come from our age or experience but from God's Word.

Notice also the biblical pattern of the public reading of Scripture and the exposition of the passage that was just read (cf. Neh. 8; Luke 4:16–30; Acts 13:13–52). Paul clearly has this pattern in mind here.

The earliest description of corporate worship we find in church history is taken from Justin Martyr's *The First Apology*. In defending what Christians practice during worship, he provides a beautiful vision of God's people gathered together:

> *On the day called Sunday, all who live in cities or in the country gather together to one place, and* the memoirs of the apostles or the writings of the prophets are read, as long as time permits; then, when the reader has finished, the president verbally

instructs, and exhorts to the imitation of these good things. *Then we all rise together and pray, and, as we before said, when our prayer is ended, bread and wine and water are brought, and the president in like manner offers prayers and thanksgivings, according to his ability, and the people assent, saying Amen; and there is a distribution to each, and a participation of that over which thanks have been given, and to those who are absent a portion is sent by the deacons. And they who are well to do, and willing, give what each thinks fit; and what is collected is deposited with the president, who succors the orphans and widows, and those who, through sickness or any other cause, are in want, and those who are in bonds, and the strangers sojourning among us, and in a word takes care of all who are in need (my emphasis).*[37]

Notice Justin's terms "instructs, and exhorts" reflect Paul's appeal in 1 Timothy 4:13. This is the historical pattern for us to follow: biblical exposition. We have the responsibility of explaining what God has said in his Word, declaring what God has done in his Son, and applying this message to the hearts of people.[38]

Exercise your gift passionately

Paul goes on to urge Timothy to use his gifts and immerse himself in the work of teaching: "Do not neglect the gift you have, which was given you by prophecy when the council of elders laid their hands on you. Practice these things, immerse yourself in them, so that all may see your progress" (4:14-15). Notice that the teaching ministry is both about *God-given ability* ("the gift") and *skill development* ("progress").

Use your gifts

Paul doesn't state what Timothy's gift is exactly, but from the context, it seems to be related to the ministry of teaching in the church. God gifts people for the ministry to which he calls them (cf. Rom. 12:6–8; 1 Cor. 12; Eph. 4:7–12; 1 Pet. 4:10–11). Like other spiritual gifts, they are for the good of the church, and so we must *use them* to build up the body (Rom. 12:6; 1 Pet. 4:10)! The gift must not be neglected.

Paul mentions some kind of prophetic message that was apparently uttered about Timothy, as well as the elders laying their hands on him (1 Tim. 4:14). This seems to be similar to Paul and Barnabas being singled out in Acts 13:1–3, where the laying on of hands is also mentioned. These elders confirmed God's gifting and calling on Timothy. Likewise, aspiring pastors should be commended by pastors who assess their lifestyle and gifting.

As church planters and pastors, we need to always "fan into flame the gift of God" (2 Tim. 1:6) and never neglect what God has given us. Aspiring pastors should seek to discern their giftings, then cultivate their gifts, and eventually use them in leadership with passion.[39]

Let them see your progress

Timothy is urged to be all in: "Practice these things, immerse yourself in them" (1 Tim. 4:15a). It's an excellent charge for us to be wholly devoted to our ministry, avoiding laziness and distraction. Rest? Yes, by all means. But when it's time to do the work, get after it.

One thing that should happen the longer you teach is that people should "see your progress" (4:15b). I'm glad this verse is in Scripture because it implies we can improve! People should see progress in our leadership (as we become more tender, a better listener, bolder, wiser, and more winsome). They should see our growth in knowledge and that we are excited about what we're learning. And they should see progress in our preaching and teaching. We should work to be clearer and more concise. We should grow in our ability both to apply the text and to address the hearts and idols of people. We need to show our progress in our ability to preach Christ from the Old Testament.

While this text is an encouragement to pastors (as it implies we can improve), it's also an important word to the congregation. They need to be reminded that pastoral leaders are still growing! They need to set realistic expectations and be patient.

I remember talking with a very well-known pastor about a paper I was writing, which focused on giving detailed analysis to his sermons. When I told him about my project, he said, "Please take recent sermons!" I appreciated that. Even the best can improve.

Examine your life and teaching persistently

Paul concludes this important passage with a sober exhortation: "Keep a close watch on yourself and on the teaching. Persist in this, for by so doing you will save both yourself and your hearers" (1 Tim 4:16). This is a summary verse for the preceding points and the entire work of pastoring.

Watch yourself

Paul gave this same word to the Ephesian elders (Acts 20:28). Watching our life involves watching our affections, for we live and speak out of the overflow of our heart (Prov. 4:23). The way we watch ourselves is by not allowing our passion for Jesus to cool. It involves drinking deeply from the wells of the gospel.

As a pastor, I must take care of my heart. I do this by doing things that nourish my soul, like reading good books, being in community, cultivating a vibrant prayer life, exercising, and resting well. Since church planting and pastoral ministry are demanding, you must be very disciplined not to be so absorbed in the work that you neglect your own spiritual life.

Watch the teaching

Every pastor is to be able to teach and keep this ministry as a top priority. We must ensure our teaching is accurate, clear, and centered on Christ. While not every elder will have the same degree of gifting, all should be able to explain and apply the text to others in a variety of contexts (such as in classes, counseling, or small groups).

Aspiring church planters should consider preparing about four to six months of sermons before launching the church. I set this idea before planters because one of the challenges, in the early days especially, will be fighting for sermon preparation time. While they won't have each one 100% finished, they can do the bulk of the interpretive work and prepare fairly detailed notes. Once the church is planted, they can add the specific application needed for their context. One might consider preparing a series through a small epistle like Philippians, Ephesians, or Colossians.

Persist in this

This aspect of Paul's exhortation is easily overlooked. Still, it's vitally important because many pastoral leaders who have fallen out of ministry have done so because they failed to give adequate attention to this part of the verse. At one time, they were watching their life and their teaching. But slowly, for various reasons, they stopped doing self-examination. And the results are tragic.

What's at stake in this persistent self-examination? Paul says, "You will save both yourself and your hearers" (1 Tim. 4:16b). We know we cannot save ourselves, for Jesus alone must do that, but Paul is speaking here of Christian endurance. It's the kind of thing he says to the Philippians: "work out your own salvation with fear and trembling" (Phil. 2:12b). Many people talk about the emotion of conversion, but the New Testament places a greater emphasis on preserving in the faith than it does on the initial emotion of conversion.[40] By perseverance in godliness and by teaching sound doctrine faithfully, Timothy will save his hearers from the dangers of false teaching, which can cause people to make a shipwreck of the faith.

Conclusion

Faithful, Christ-exalting exposition of Scripture is central to the health and vitality of the church. God has given pastoral leaders a unique ability to teach so that they may instruct, bless, exhort, and protect God's people. While the ability to teach is a gift from God, it is also a skill that pastors should seek to develop. A faithful shepherd seeks to exemplify his teaching personally, expound the Scriptures publicly, exercise his gift passionately, and examine his life and teaching persistently.

Reflection questions

1. What is your philosophy of preaching? Why? How do you prepare a sermon? How would you go about preparing a sermon plan for three to six months?

2. Can you think of a time where you were able to rightly discern false doctrine and lovingly rebuke

a brother, bringing him into alignment with the truth of God's Word (Tit. 1:9)?

3. How does seeing any particular text through the lens of the whole Bible's redemptive narrative help you rightly understand and teach it?

4. Can you demonstrate your ability to teach with one of these difficult and often misappropriated texts: Jeremiah 29:11–13; John 15:1; Romans 8:28; 1 Timothy 2:3–4; or Hebrews 6:4–8?

11

An Entrepreneurial Aptitude

I have been listening to a podcast called *How I Built This* (from National Park Radio). The host, Guy Raz, interviews leading entrepreneurs and innovators, digging into the stories behind their companies and movements. I've learned about the backstory of Sub Pop Records, Shake Shack, Fitbit, Sierra Nevada, and Five Guys, just to name a handful. It didn't take long to detect that these entrepreneurs have several things in common with church planters.

Webster defines *entrepreneurial* as "having to do with the creation and development of economic ventures."[41] As a church planter, we're not about the creation and development of economic ventures, but about the creation and development of new gospel ventures (for example, creating evangelistic initiatives, developing discipleship models, and starting new churches).

Church planters with entrepreneurial *aptitude* share many of the same abilities as other entrepreneurs.

Good church planters are characterized by *passion*. This includes being a self-starter. It means being a disciplined, hard worker.

Additionally, effective church planters are *resourceful*. I often say, "Former drug dealers make good church planters!" (emphasis on "former"!). What I mean is that they're streetwise and savvy. They know how to get things done with few resources.

Further, successful church planters display *flexibility and creativity* based on their context and opportunities. They cast a compelling vision, develop clear plans for reaching their specific area, and constantly evaluate their work, learning and making adjustments.

Moreover, effective church planters *gather people*. They can recruit others to join in the new work, including other leaders who are gifted in ways they aren't. They build trust within their teams. They can also appeal to outsiders in a compelling way.

Finally, good church planters give *attention to practical details*. These include matters like childcare, security, parking, legal issues, fundraising, handling finances, building needs, details concerning corporate worship, communication, and so on. While they usually work with others on these issues, they don't let them go unchecked.

If a fruitful church planter was on *How I Built This*, chances are that many of these traits would be mentioned. But the Christian leader understands behind our "building" is Jesus' promise to build his church (Matt. 16:18). Christ, our Savior, gives us the abilities and opportunities, and strengthens us for his work in the world. So we can only boast in the Lord as the church grows and bears much fruit (1 Cor. 1:31; 3:6).

Biblical reflections

Admittedly, of all the competencies discussed, *entrepreneurial aptitude* is the hardest to support from Scripture. We read about very clear requirements, like you "must be above reproach" and "able to teach" (1 Tim. 3:2), but we don't have a verse that says, "You must be entrepreneurial." However, much of the way I understand this competency is under the umbrella of *faithful stewardship*.

As image bearers of God, we have been given the abilities to create and work for God's glory (Gen. 1:26). We are to use all of our God-given abilities and resources to make the most of our God-given opportunities for the sake of the gospel. This means we should give attention to the pragmatic aspects of church planting. Being a theologically driven planter/pastor doesn't mean you shouldn't think about all the practical ways you can make a kingdom impact. Allow me to pull a few biblical threads together on this idea of faithfully using all that God gives us for gospel purposes.

Proverbs on work

The book of Proverbs is full of concise, pithy sayings about diligence, industry, and hard work. A life lived to God's glory just doesn't happen. It requires thoughtful study, discipline, and godly ambition.

We are instructed on the one hand to avoid the sluggard's way of life! The sluggard is characterized by a number of unflattering traits: *indolence, inactivity, idleness, apathy, helplessness, harmfulness, excuse-making, procrastination, emptiness, and arrogance* (see Prov. 10:26; 13:4; 15:19; 20:4; 21:25–26; 24:30–34; 26:14–16). Sluggards don't plant churches! On the other hand, we are instructed to "consider" the ant in order to be wise (Prov. 6:6–11). Imagine the thought—being taught by a bug! But the ant gives a much better picture than the sluggard, illustrating what it looks like to work wisely, diligently, and taking initiative in every season.

This emphasis on diligence reflects the value of work in the opening chapters of Genesis, where work is seen as a privilege and responsibility, and as something expressing God's creativity (Gen. 1–2; Ps. 104:23). While the fall has made all work more difficult (Gen. 3:19; Eccl. 2:18–23), it hasn't canceled the view of seeing our work as a gift and as something we must do with diligence. Proverbs expresses this high view of work in various ways, like speaking of the reward of diligence: "Whoever works his land will have plenty of bread, but he who follows worthless pursuits lacks sense" (12:11) and, "The plans of the diligent lead surely to abundance, but everyone who is hasty comes only to poverty" (21:5).

Church planting is hard work. Paul compares ministry to being a soldier, an athlete, and a farmer (2. Tim 2:1–7). We're not rock stars; we're more like farmers. We wake up, plant the gospel, and beg God to send the rain.

Paul says elsewhere that leaders should lead with "zeal" (Rom. 12:8). I've read many biographies of prominent entrepreneurs and Christian leaders, and none of them were lazy. We must guard against overwork and burnout. However, what I see today in my context is not the problem of overwork but the problems of entitlement and lack of diligence.

Ecclesiastes on toil and wise industry
While the writer of Ecclesiastes ("the Preacher," 1:1) laments the many difficulties of life, he often speaks of the value of work. We're urged to throw ourselves into the tasks of life with energy and confidence. The preacher tells us about the difficulties in toil and the danger of overworking and having the wrong motives (4:4–8). Yet he states that we can still find enjoyment in our faithful labor (cf. 2:24; 3:13; 5:18–20; 8:15; 9:10).

Further, the preacher also calls us to live by faith in this life, with application given to the merchant's ventures and the farmer (11:1–6). Regarding the merchant, he says, "Cast your bread upon the waters, for you will find it after many days" (11:1). This is an expression that most likely speaks of international trade. Merchants are being urged to send out their goods on seven or eight ships, diversifying their investments because some of them are bound to bring back a return: "Give a portion to seven, or even to eight, for you know not what disaster may happen on earth" (11:2). In context, the preacher is saying to the businessman, "Don't allow the unpredictability of life to make you careless or paralyzed with fear, but live by faith, wisdom, and patience."

Phil Ryken applies the preacher's words about the merchant to the world of ministry:

> Rather than holding on to what we have, hoarding it all for ourselves—which is the error that the man with one talent made in a parable that Jesus told (Matthew 25:24–28)—God invites us to be venture capitalists for the kingdom of God ... It is about having the holy boldness to do seven (or even eight) things to spread the gospel and then waiting for God's ship to come in. Some of the things that we attempt may fail (or at least seem to fail at the time)—some of the ministries we start, for example, or the churches we plant, or the efforts we make to share the good news of the cross and the empty tomb. But we should never stop investing with the gospel in as many places as we can. Whenever we engage in kingdom enterprises, we offer the Holy Spirit something he can and often will use to save people's souls.[42]

Indeed, we want to cast the gospel in as many places as we can, in as many ways as we can, and trust God to bring in the ships. Gospel movements have historically happened not only through the renewal of gospel preaching but also through creative mission, like the use of the printing press, songwriting, various types of evangelism, and contextualized ministries.

The parable of the talents

In Jesus' parable of the talents (Matt. 25:14–30), we find another biblical example of being faithful stewards of all we're given (see also Luke 19:11–27 for a similar parable). A talent was worth about twenty years of a laborer's wages and represents specific privileges and opportunities for kingdom work. The first servant with five talents, and the second servant with two talents, took what was given to them, acted industrially, and earned a return (Matt. 25:16–17). They receive a "Well done" from the Master and are promised greater responsibility and stewardship in the life to come (25:20–23). However, the third servant took his one talent and hid it in the ground (25:24–25). He displayed laziness, fear, and poor stewardship, and consequently met the Master's wrath (25:26–30). Jesus also adds that using our God-given abilities faithfully (like servants one and two) will result in further opportunities for kingdom work (25:29). So let us be faithful with all we have in view of the coming of our Master.

Paul the church planter

Not only was Paul a tentmaker who knew the world of business, but his ministry also displayed many of the traits previously discussed. Missiologist Ed Stetzer notes nine characteristics of Paul the church planter, his third point being: "Paul was an entrepreneurial leader."[43] He then lists examples:

- *He had a vision and call from God (Acts 9:15; Rom. 15:20–23).*

- *His vision was to be the apostle to the Gentiles by leading missionary teams into new territories to plant churches. He combined quick-strike evangelism with church planting. The wedding of these two powerful methodologies sparked movements that made an impact for generations.*

- *He selected workers and apprentices he wanted on his team. He was not afraid to ask others to make sacrifices for the cause of Christ (Acts 16:2–3). Sometimes, he would not let people on his team (15:38). Paul also appointed long-term leaders for the churches he started (14:23). He even gave direction to his teammates as to where they should minister (18:19; 19:22).*

- *He received direction from God about where his team should plant, and his teammates had confidence in his decisions (16:6–10).*

- *He was a proactive strategist (13:14, 44–49). He established a reproducible pattern for his church planting (14:1; 17:2). [This involved teaching in the synagogues first when arriving in a city.]*

- *He deliberately did advanced planning (19:21).*

- *He was a flexible, risk-taking pioneer (1 Cor. 9:19–21).[44]*

Martin Luther and the Reformation

Allow me to draw attention to Martin Luther's example again, but this time for a different reason. Noted historian Andrew Pettegree has an excellent book called *Brand Luther: 1517, Printing, and the Making of the Reformation*, in which he highlights the often-overlooked aspect of Luther's leadership. He shows that Luther was not simply a great theologian and preacher, but a world-class master of mass communication. Through his short pamphlets, written in colloquial German style and illustrated by the artist Lucas Cranach, as well as his use of the printing press, Luther sparked the Reformation.

Luther turned his small town into a center of publishing. Pettegree notes, "Luther was no distracted intellectual, but a man of great practical skill ... He spent his whole life in and out of the print shops, observing and directing. He had very firm views on how books should look ... [he] understood the aesthetics of the book."[45] He adds, "Luther and his friends used every instrument of communication known to medieval and Renaissance Europe: correspondence, song, word of mouth, painted and printed images."[46]

Note that while Luther recovered the gospel of justification by faith alone, the message needed to be heralded, and he found every way possible to do so. He was not just a theologian; he was someone with cultural awareness, the ability to work with his friends, a deep work ethic, an appreciation of art and music, and some business acumen, especially around the printing press.

Pettegree further comments, "the Reformation could not have occurred as it did without print. Print propelled Martin Luther, a man who had published nothing in the first thirty years of his life, to instant celebrity."[47] While Luther wasn't trying to be a celebrity, and while that must never be our desire, the point is clear: his gospel ambition led him to use every possible means of communication available to him.

Finally, Pettegree summarizes, "It is these two stories, the spiritual and theological, and the economic and commercial, that need to be woven together to understand the extraordinary impact of the Reformation. In this way, Wittenberg, the small border town perched on the edge of civilization, would share with Luther the responsibility for igniting one of the great transforming movements of the last millennium."[48] This historical example should enliven minds to imagine what ways we may seek to communicate the gospel in our modern world.

Church planters must first and foremost know the gospel and center everything on it, for it is of "first importance" (1 Cor. 15:3). But such a life-changing message should also move us to use every resource we have and seize every opportunity before us to make it known to everyone. Let us cast our bread on the waters, believing that the Word of God does not return void.

As a planter, you cannot do it all, but you should always consider your capacity, gifts, and opportunities, and seek to put them to kingdom use as good stewards of the Master. This may mean writing, blogging, podcasting, making great videos, preaching at your church and other venues in the city, training pastors, and helping to plant churches locally and globally. Let us do everything we can to spread the gospel and build up Christ's church. This is a great time to be a spiritual entrepreneur, to start something new, to sow the Word of God in as many ways as we can, trusting God to bring in the ships. Jesus Christ is the Lord of the harvest who is gathering a people for himself. If he used Martin Luther in a backwater town to start the Reformation, what might he do with faithful, creative, innovative stewards today?

Conclusion

Church planters with entrepreneurial aptitude have the skills to start and develop new gospel works. They are marked by characteristics like passion, hard work, and resourcefulness. They have the ability to gather people, cast vision, and give attention to practical details. They are flexible and creative as they consider how to engage various contexts with the gospel. In short, they are faithful stewards of all God has given them, and they make the most of the opportunities before them.

Reflection questions

1. How does the concept of being faithful, creative, and innovative stewards reframe our understanding of spiritual entrepreneurship in church planting?

2. Have you ever started something from nothing? How did you go about it? What did you learn from that experience?

3. How would you describe your Spirit-wrought strategic plan for planting a church?

4. Consider the example of Paul. How would you go about selecting others to form a team in this gospel endeavor? What gifts are you looking for in those you hope to recruit?

Conclusion

Though not technically a "pastoral epistle," one can see 2 Corinthians in a very similar way, especially the first six chapters where Paul explains and defends his ministry. He opens his heart wide to the Corinthians (2 Cor. 6:11) as he explains his motives and his message.

Paul founded this church some six or seven years previously, but the relationship was not ideal. He was facing much criticism led by a group of "super-apostles." They accused Paul of suffering too much to be an apostle, of having impure motives, of not having good speaking abilities, of not being evangelistically successful, and for not having letters of recommendation vouching for his legitimacy.

In the middle of this first major section of the letter, Paul says twice, "We do not lose heart" (2 Cor. 4:1, 16). Apparently, losing heart crossed Paul's mind. And if it crossed his mind, it will certainly cross ours!

We tell our aspiring church planters, "We want to prepare you for a thirty-year run!" Sadly, many start well but don't finish well. So what will keep us going? How can we be faithful to the end?

Ministry leaders throughout history have gone through difficult seasons. After his initial encounter with Pharaoh, Moses asked God, "Why did you ever send me?" (Ex. 5:22). God proceeded to encourage Moses with his promises, which provided the needed strength to persevere. After Elijah won a mighty victory at Mount Carmel, we find him, in the very next chapter, weak and discouraged, sitting under a broom tree, and asking God to take his life (1 Kgs 19:4ff)! But God graciously renewed his servant, and the next time we see Elijah, he is bold and courageous (21:17–24).

Charles Spurgeon suffered from a burning kidney disease, gout, rheumatism, and more. Stress took its toll on the Prince of Preachers, who said, "I become so perplexed that I sink in heart, and dream that it were better for me to have never been born than to have been called to bear all this multitude upon my heart."[49] Even so, he believed in God's sovereign purposes, that these trials made him a more compassionate pastor (cf. 2 Cor. 1:3–7), and that the Lord used these trials to keep him humble and dependent on the Lord's grace (cf. 2 Cor. 12:10). Spurgeon said, "Those who are honored of their Lord in public, have usually to endure a secret chastening, or to carry a peculiar cross, lest by any means they exalt themselves, and fall into the snare of the devil."[50]

The good news is God uses weak and even troubled people, "jars of clay" (2 Cor. 4:7), who make the glory of the gospel known. How did Paul keep going when he felt burdened by life and ministry challenges? He says,

"Therefore, having this ministry by the mercy of God, we do not lose heart" (2 Cor. 4:1). Notice he draws attention to *the mercy of God*. Gospel ministry is challenging, and church planting is extremely hard, but we persevere by thinking deeply on God's mercy. Paul recognizes it's all mercy. His salvation is owing to God's mercy (cf. 1 Tim. 1:16; Eph. 2:4). And his ministry isn't earned either, but has been granted to him out of the sheer mercy and kindness of God.

What kept Paul going will keep us going: the nature of the gospel itself and the nature of gospel ministry. Ministry success won't keep us going. If only success motivates you, then when you "fail," you're toast. Popularity won't keep us going. Don't ever allow being noticed to drive you. Influence in the political arena won't keep us going either—most of us will have no direct political influence. These are weak motivations. We need a bigger engine to have a marathon ministry. We must never forget the gospel—what God has done for us and is doing in us keeps us going as we look into the future.

As those who have a ministry by the mercy of God, we need to remember—especially in hard seasons—that our sins are forgiven! Christ's righteousness is ours! We have a conscious sprinkled clean by the blood of the Lamb! The Spirit of God is in us, empowering us, and guaranteeing the glory that awaits us! Before we are ministry leaders, we are adopted sons and daughters of God!

Church-planting friend, I tell you affectionately what a good friend told me recently while we were discussing our personal ministries: "We should be in hell, bro." But we're not! God has had mercy on us. Wake up every morning and meditate on the good news for the good of your soul, your family, and your church.

We get to preach the gospel and minister in Jesus' name. May the nature of the gospel itself and the privilege of doing gospel ministry cause us to ever stand amazed. May they regularly renew us for the work until we see Jesus and enjoy all that the new creation will bring.

Bibliography

Bird, Michael F., *Romans* in The Story of God Bible Commentary (Grand Rapids: Zondervan, 2016).

Carson, D. A., *Scandalous* (Wheaton: Crossway, 2010).

Dever, Mark., *Discipling* (Wheaton: Crossway, 2016).

Diehl, Judith A., *2 Corinthians* in The Story of God Bible Commentary (Grand Rapids: Zondervan, 2020).

Doriani, Daniel M., *1 Peter* in The Reformed Expository Commentary (Phillipsburg: P&R, 2014).

Keller, Timothy, *Center Church* (Grand Rapids: Zondervan, 2012).

Keller, Timothy, "Ministry and Character," available online at https://redeemercitytocity.com/articles-stories/ministry-and-character (accessed February 4, 2021).

Keller, Timothy J. and J. Allen Thompson, *Church Planter Manual* (New York: Redeemer Church Planting Center, 2002).

Knight III, George W., *The Pastoral Epistles* in The New International Greek Testament Commentary (Grand

Rapids: Eerdmans, 1992).

Merida, Tony, *Christ-Centered Exposition: Exalting Jesus in Ephesians* (Nashville: B&H, 2014).

Merida, Tony, *The Christ-Centered Expositor* (Nashville: B&H, 2016).

Merida, Tony, *Love Your Church* (The Good Book Company, 2021).

Merida, Tony, *Ordinary* (Nashville: B&H, 2015).

Pettegree, Andrew, *Brand Luther* (New York: Penguin, 2016).

Powlison, David, *Safe and Sound: Standing Firm in Spiritual Battles* (Greensboro: New Growth Press, 2019).

Reeves, Michael, *Spurgeon on the Christian Life* (Wheaton: Crossway, 2018).

Ryken, Philip Graham, *Ecclesiastes* in Preaching the Word (Wheaton: Crossway, 2010).

Spurgeon, Charles, *Lectures to My Students* (Reprint; Grand Rapids: Zondervan, 1954).

Stetzer, Ed, *Planting Missional Churches* (Nashville: B&H, 2006).

Stott, John, *Guard the Truth* (Downers Grove: InterVarsity Press, 1996).

Tice, Rico, *Faithful Leaders* (The Good Book Company, 2021).

Webber, Robert E., *Ancient-Future* Worship (Grand Rapids: Baker, 2008).

Witmer, Timothy Z., *The Shepherd Leader* (Phillipsburg: P&R, 2010).

Wright, Christopher J. H., *Sweeter than Honey: Preaching Christ from the Old Testament* (Carlisle: Langham Preaching Resources, 2015), p. 18.

Endnotes

Introduction

1   Tim Keller identifies *eighteen* characteristics of
     a church planter: (1) prayer, (2) spiritual vitality,
     (3) integrity, (4) God's call, (5) family life, (6)
     conscientiousness, (7) humility, (8) leadership, (9)
     evangelism, (10) management, (11) preaching, (12)
     [contextualized] philosophy of ministry, (13) training
     leaders, (14) flexibility, (15) likeability, (16) emotional
     stability, (17) sensitivity, and (18) dynamism. He also
     lists *nine* characteristics of the planter's spouse (if
     married): (1) family life, (2) integrity, (3) God's call,
     (4) spiritual vitality, (5) prayer, (6) role [as spouse and
     leader/role model], (7) cooperation, (8) sensitivity,
     and (9) emotional stability. See Timothy J. Keller
     and J. Allen Thompson, *Church Planter Manual*
     (New York: Redeemer Church Planting Center,
     2002), pp. 69–70.

2   Unless otherwise noted, all Scripture references are
     taken from the English Standard Bible (Wheaton:
     Crossway, 2016).

1. Spiritual Vitality

3   David Powlison outlines the following points about spiritual warfare. First, spiritual warfare is a metaphor for standing on the Lord's side in the epic struggle between the Lord and his enemies. Second, spiritual warfare is a moral struggle. Third, spiritual warfare is a synonym for the struggles of the Christian life. Finally, spiritual warfare is a battle for lordship. See *Safe and Sound: Standing Firm in Spiritual Battles* (Greensboro: New Growth Press, 2019), pp. 13–14.

4   Timothy J. Keller and J. Allen Thompson, *Church Planter Manual*, p. 10.

5   Judith A. Diehl, *2 Corinthians* in The Story of God Bible Commentary (Grand Rapids: Zondervan, 2020), 105.

2. Theological Clarity

6   D .A. Carson, *Scandalous* (Wheaton: Crossway, 2010), p. 11.

7   Timothy Keller, *Center Church* (Grand Rapids: Zondervan, 2012), p. 40.

8   Quoted on Twitter on March 27, 2020.

9   Credit to my friend Landon Dowden for this illustration.

10 Christopher J. H. Wright, *Sweeter than Honey: Preaching Christ from the Old Testament* (Carlisle:

Langham Preaching Resources, 2015), p. 18. The graphic here has been slightly adapted from the one in Wright's book.

11 Ibid.

12 Ibid., p. 20.

13 Craig Bartholomew and Michael Goheen, *The Drama of Scripture: Finding Our Place in the Biblical Story* (second edition; London: SPCK, 2016); Vaughan Roberts, *God's Big Picture* (Nottingham: Inter-Varsity Press, 2009); Sally Lloyd-Jones, *The Jesus Storybook Bible* (Grand Rapids: Zondervan, 2007).

14 This is an analogy from my friend Bryan Chapell.

15 Michael F. Bird, *Romans* in The Story of God Bible Commentary (Grand Rapids: Zondervan, 2016), p. 32.

3. Conviction and Commendation

16 Adam Muhtaseb, "The Secret to Church Planting (From a Former Muslim)," an article available at https://www.thegospelcoalition.org/article/secret-church-planting/ (accessed March 16, 2021).

17 John Piper, "A Holy Ambition," a sermon available at https://www.desiringgod.org/messages/holy-ambition--2 (accessed March 15, 2021).

18 Ibid.

19   Tom Schreiner, "Proclaiming the Gospel to the Ends of the Earth," a sermon available at https://www.cliftonbaptist.org/sermons-and-audio/sermon/2013-01-20/proclaiming-the-gospel-to-the-ends-of-the-earth (accessed March 15, 2021).

20   Charles Spurgeon, *Lectures to My Students,* (reprint; Grand Rapids: Zondervan, 1954), pp. 26–27.

21   Timothy J. Keller and J. Allen Thompson, *Church Planter Manual*, p. 68.

4. A Healthy Marriage

22   John Stott, *Involvement: Social and Sexual Relationships in the Modern World*, volume 2 (Old Tappan, New Jersey: Fleming H. Revell, 1984), p. 163.

5. Healthy Relationships

23   Charles Spurgeon, *Lectures to My Students*, pp. 168–69.

6. Godly Leadership

24   Tim Z. Witmer, *The Shepherd Leader* (Phillipsburg: P&R, 2010), p. 189.

25   Daniel M. Doriani, *1 Peter* in the Reformed Expository Commentary (Phillipsburg: P&R, 2014), p. 211.

26   John Stott, *Guard the Truth* (Downers Grove: InterVarsity Press, 1996), p. 120.

7. Spiritual Maturity

27 This third point was made well in an article by Tim Keller, "Ministry and Character," available online at https://redeemercitytocity.com/articles-stories/ministry-and-character (accessed February 4, 2021).

28 In Rico Tice, *Faithful Leaders* (The Good Book Company, 2021), p. 45.

8. Missional Lifestyle

29 Rodney Stark, *Cities of God* (New York: HarperCollins, 2007), pp. 13–14

30 See my book *Love Your Church* for more on Peter's instructions and our witness (The Good Book Company, 2021), pp. 125–26.

31 Portions of this chapter on network evangelism and on hospitality have appeared on our Acts 29 blog. I have also written about hospitality in my book *Ordinary* (Nashville: B&H, 2015).

9. Disciple-Making

32 Mark Dever defines "discipling" simply as "helping others follow Jesus." See his book *Discipling* (Wheaton: Crossway, 2016), p. 13.

33 This story is taken from Sinclair Ferguson in an audio sermon of his that I once heard.

10. The Ability to Teach

34 See Andrew Pettegree, *Brand Luther* (New York: Penguin, 2016), pp. 143–63.

35 George W. Knight III, *The Pastoral Epistles* in The New International Greek Testament Commentary (Grand Rapids: Eerdmans, 1992), p. 205.

36 John Stott, *Guard the Truth*, p. 120.

37 Taken from Robert E. Webber, *Ancient-Future Worship* (Grand Rapids: Baker, 2008), pp. 92–93.

38 Tony Merida, *The Christ-Centered Expositor* (Nashville: B&H, 2016), p. 16.

39 John Stott, *Guard the Truth*, p. 123.

40 Ibid., p. 124.

11. An Entrepreneurial Attitude

41 See Merriam-Webster online dictionary at https://www.merriam-webster.com/dictionary/ entrepreneurialism (accessed March 9, 2021).

42 Philip Graham Ryken, *Ecclesiastes* in Preaching the Word (Wheaton: Crossway, 2010), p. 256.

43 Ed Stetzer, *Planting Missional Churches* (Nashville: B&H, 2006), p. 45.

44 Ibid., pp. 45–46. The last bullet point is actually stated as Stetzer's fifth of nine points, but I included it here as I see this as a mark of an entrepreneurial leader.

45 Andrew Pettegree, *Brand Luther*, p. xiii.

46 Ibid., p. 11.

47 Ibid., p. 11.

48 Ibid., pp. 24–25.

Conclusion

49 Taken from Michael Reeves, *Spurgeon on the Christian Life* (Wheaton: Crossway, 2018), p. 163.

50 Ibid., p. 164.